Praise for I'M MOVING from Realtors® and Brokers

Awesome!! The facts you need and the emotional sensitivity you appreciate.
> Norm Erickson: Realtor®, Broker, Real Estate Instructor

Bill Peter's enthusiasm and the passionate way he writes are wonderful. Very informative and easy reading.
> Julie Olson: Realtor®, Broker

Realtors®, this book is a treasure to share with every client. It is sure to generate referrals. Thanks, Bill.
> Carol Martin: Realtor®, Real Estate Instructor

Great book!! I'M MOVING could be the best referral producer ever for real estate agents.
> Dale Couet: Realtor®

A "must read" for anyone buying or selling a home; all you need to know in one book.
> Mark DeKarske: Realtor®, Real Estate Instructor

With Bill Peter's book in hand, ask your prospective Realtors®, "How will you reduce or eliminate my anxiety of buying or selling a home?"
> Larry Stoller: Broker, Owner

For PEACE-OF-MIND during the real estate experience, I'M MOVING is a "must read."
> Steve Stewart: Realtor®, Real Estate Trainer

"I'M MOVING"

"Eliminating the anxiety of buying or selling a home."

"It has been my passion to create a fun-to-read real estate book with very reliable information, which is also emotionally uplifting."

Bill Peter

"I'M MOVING"

© 1998 by Bill Peter. No part of this book may be reproduced by any mechanical, photographic or electronic process, or in the form of an audio recording, nor may be stored in a retrieval system, transmitted, or otherwise copied for public or private use without written permission of the author and publisher.

All rights reserved.
ISBN 1-890676-26-8

Printed in the United States of America.

3rd Printing
Library of Congress Catalog Card Number: 98-86808

Beaver's Pond Press

3 4 5 02 01 00 99

"I'M MOVING"

"Eliminating the anxiety of buying or selling a home."

Bill Peter

"I'M MOVING"

TABLE OF CONTENTS

Page

Introduction
- About the cover — 9
- Dedication — 10
- Thanks to my supporters — 11
- I'M MOVING overview — 12
- How to read I'M MOVING — 13

Emotional Issues
1. Yesterday, today and tomorrow — 15
2. Never too old to move — 19
3. Making a house a home — 23
4. Coping with the emotions of moving — 29
5. A new job opportunity — 33

The Best Time to Buy and Sell
6. The economy — 39
7. Location, location, location — 45
8. A time to sell and a time to buy — 55
9. Win-win negotiations — 59

Selecting an Agent
10. Suggestions on selecting someone to market your home — 65
11. The real estate broker and the real estate agent — 69
12. Tips for the buyer — 73
13. Your time is valuable — 79
14. Forms, forms and more forms — 83
15. Your comfortable home is probably not ready to sell — 85

TABLE OF CONTENTS (continued)

                                                                                 Page

Financial Issues
16 What price home can I qualify for?   91
17 Mortgages and monthly payments   95
18 Shopping for a mortgage   99
19 Sales commissions   103
20 Roger's remodeling adventure   107
21 The title and title insurance   109
22 The wisdom of a home inspection   113

More Emotional Issues
23 Michelle moves to Florida   127
24 Tears of sadness and joy   131
25 What is your work? Is it real estate? 135
26 Retirement communities, etc.   137
27 Divorce and moving   141
28 What's important in life anyhow?   145

Practical Exercise
29 A Workbook Section   149

Summary
30 Summary of I'M MOVING   159
31 I'M MOVING feedback from readers   163
32 Order form for more copies of I'M MOVING 165

Appendix
33 Quotes on PEACE-OF-MIND   167
34 About the author   171

About the Cover

The goal of I'M MOVING is to eliminate the anxiety of moving and to provide PEACE-OF-MIND to those who are in the process of buying or selling a home.

The double rainbow - our comforting symbol of I'M MOVING - symbolizes happiness and peace. The rainbow appears with beauty and flair. The beginning and the end of the rainbow are not always clear to the observer, just like the process of moving. A double rainbow is a good luck omen; good luck comes because we have prepared ourselves well to enjoy the moving process with the help of real estate professionals.

> We visualize the double rainbow over us and the feeling of peace in our heart as we, through contemplation and imagination, have transformed the potentially stressful scenario of moving into a peaceful and joyful experience.

We visualize the double rainbow over us and the feeling of peace in our heart as we, through contemplation and imagination, have transformed the potentially stressful scenario of moving into a peaceful and joyful experience.

"I'M MOVING"

Dedication

Dedicated to my children: Gail, Todd, Kenneth and David. The family moves were always a challenge and the children made as many difficult adjustments as their parents...physically and certainly emotionally.

The states we lived in together, or are now living in, are: New York, Massachusetts, Maine, Delaware, Virginia, Tennessee, Alabama, Michigan, Minnesota, Ohio, Florida, Oregon and Colorado. I have lived in nineteen homes to date.

INTRODUCTION

Thanks To My Supporters

I'M MOVING was fun to write. It was written, edited and assembled with the help and support of many people.

Special thanks to my wife, Arlene, for her patience and support. Graphics, design and production were wonderful contributions of Ryan Soderstrom and Milt Adams. Draft after draft of the words were made possible through the excellent help of Virginia Matzinger.

Suggestions for improvement on the early drafts were extremely valuable from Joann Buie, Chris Cahill, Dale Couet, Mark DeKarske, Alyssa Depesa, Norm Erickson, Marilyn Everett, Bill Gerst, Peggy Hemple, Don Keller, Carol Martin, Julie Olson, Kenneth Peter, Stephen Stewart, and Larry Stoller.

Thanks to all for the great encouragement and support.

I'M MOVING OVERVIEW

I'M MOVING offers the promise of helping people eliminate the anxiety of buying or selling a home. Instead of the negative emotions of anxiety, the goal is the positive results of PEACE-OF-MIND.

The uniqueness of this book is that it captures in one place:

a. Valuable information about the financial side of real estate transactions to remove much of the mystery,
b. Useful advice on how you can quickly become more knowledgeable, and then find a real estate agent you can TRUST,
c. Helpful evaluations of the significant emotional side of moving and
d. Careful attention to the important aspects of moving and buying or selling a home as they impact both the left and right sides of your brain (logic and information/emotions and imagination).

I'M MOVING was designed to be a fun book to meet the needs of people at a time of high stress. In addition to useful information and advice, you will find many fascinating graphics, poems, etc. to heighten your imagination.

INTRODUCTION

How to Read *I'M MOVING*

Most people will start on the next page and just read to the end. However, if you are curious about the mortgage chapters, start there. Or, maybe the emotions of your family are your biggest concern...start there. If divorce is on your mind...start there. Wherever you start, each chapter is easy to understand by itself. Skip around, have fun, and get informed in your own pattern of reading.

"I'm Moving"

Emotional Issues

1. Yesterday, today, and tomorrow
2. Never too old to move
3. Making a house a home
4. Coping with the emotions of moving
5. A new job opportunity

1

Yesterday, Today, And Tomorrow

The last words my mother said to me, on her deathbed in the hospital at age 85, were, "Bill, I'm going home." She closed her eyes, turned her head and took her last breath.

My dad and I were well aware that the end was near, sadly he was out of the room that particular minute.

> People can alter their lives by altering their attitudes.
> William James

It was a peaceful death for my mom after battling cancer for two years. In those last two years, she had created opportunities to see all the members of her family and gradually to give away her various possessions to those who she felt would enjoy each item the most. She was separating herself from her possessions while celebrating her relationships with family members.

Home to her was a place of safety, comfort and nurturing and she looked forward to her final home in heaven as a peaceful place.

The lesson from my mom to me was a powerful one. Material possessions are to be enjoyed but only the memories, relationships and love are truly of lasting value over time – eternal.

To this day, my mom is often part of my dreams, as is my dad

(I called him pop). Mom and pop. In a recent dream, mom, pop and I were involved in a group hug, our three heads touching and taking turns talking, hugging and kissing each other. My mom and pop are still with me in my memory and my soul. Death changes some things but love and memories go way beyond the grave.

A home should be a place of safety, comfort and nurturing, a place for PEACE-OF-MIND.

Our experiences of "Yesterday" are an important influence on our decisions of "Today" as we visualize the "Tomorrows" of our life.

A home is more than a building, furniture and land. A home is filled with love, joy and dreams...and, yes, some sadness and disappointments. The home or homes that you and I grew up in as children are buildings, furniture and land but, more importantly,...memories, relationships and love. A home is a safe place (for most people). If it is not safe, we want to leave to find a safe place.

The buying or selling of a home is a very emotional experience. Some cry and some say "good riddance." The memories from the happy times and good relationships in the home are ones we cherish.

As we dream of our new home, we visualize a peaceful, fun place. Maybe with beautiful trees, water nearby, a beautiful flower garden, a cozy kitchen, a fireplace, a luxurious spa for a bathroom, a neighborhood with a lot of children, or maybe a quiet farm with horses nearby. If your home is for one or two people, you have different thoughts about your space needs than if you have seven people in your family and twenty-seven close relatives nearby.

As we dream about our new home, we think of our "Yesterdays" and visualize the "Tomorrows" we hope to experience. Our emotional comfort is extremely important in the purchase or sale of a home. Sure, a home is the biggest single investment in dollars, which most people make; more importantly, it involves a decision where safety, comfort and nurturing need to play big roles.

Forever Home: A Real Estate Cycle

Our first home is our mother's womb - safe,

comfortable and nurturing, and

Our final home is heaven for eternity - safe,

comfortable and nurturing.

We live life between womb and eternity in a series of

environments that we call home.

Our home is with our parents as we grow from infancy

through childhood into adulthood.

The first home of our own provides a sense of freedom

- a small apartment

which is what we can barely afford.

As our income increases and we want friends

"I'M MOVING"

or a spouse to join us,
we seek a larger apartment, a townhome
or a small individual home.
We often are blessed with children and desire a larger
house to make our home,
and we think back to when we lived with our parents.
More children or a move to a new city for work,
and we want a larger house, and so on, and so on.
But children grow and leave and get
married and we have more
house than we want to care for,
And sometimes we are alone as the result of death or
divorce and the house seems too large.
We yearn for a comfortable, smaller home which is not
as much work to maintain.
Then, as we get older, a home of our own is not practical
and we move to a retirement community, an assisted living
facility and, very reluctantly, to a nursing home.
Our freedom is decreased near the end as we look toward a
place to live which is safe, comfortable and nurturing.
It's fascinating but true, this is the real estate cycle
of our lives between womb and eternity.
Let us mark this real estate cycle well and make it safe,
comfortable and nurturing.

2
Never Too Old To Move

> The future belongs to those who believe in the beauty of their dreams.
> *Eleanor Roosevelt*

Sometimes we need a large home, other times a small one. The transition can occur at 20, 30, 40, 50, 60, 70, or 80. Our needs change as family size changes. Our desires change as we have a growing financial nest egg, a better job and a desire for a larger or more luxurious home. Sometimes, we elect to move to a smaller home.

The cost of housing is dramatically different in different parts of the country, rural or urban, etc. A home with 4,000 square feet can be found in some parts of the country for $200,000 and in other parts of the country for $400,000. In a major city, a condominium of just 1,500 square feet can sell for $400,000. The same wide range of prices exists for all sizes of homes.

The city in which you are employed often determines the approximate area where you will live. A majority of people live within ten miles of their work. It is very important to check housing costs

"I'M MOVING"

among cities if you are considering employment in several different cities. Sometimes a great job offer in dollars does not look quite as attractive after considering housing costs, commuting expenses, taxes, etc. It is a balancing act in many cases.

But life is not only about money. What cultural features, schools, sports, recreation, etc., does one community offer vs. another?

In a lifetime, most people move several times. The key is to look at change as an opportunity, a time for excitement and new experiences. A time for the adventure of "what next" at any age.

Forever Young

Youth is not a time of life: it is a state of mind.

It is a temper of the will, a quality of the imagination,

a vigor of the emotions.

Nobody grows old merely by living a number of years.

People grow old only by deserting their ideals.

Years wrinkle the skin, but to give up enthusiasm

wrinkles the soul.

EMOTIONAL ISSUES

Worry, doubt, self-distrust, fear and despair - -

these are the long, long years that bow the heart

and turn the greening spirit back to dust.

Whether nine or ninety, there is in every human being's

heart the lure of wonder,

the undaunted challenge of events,

the unfailing childlike appetite for what next,

and the joy of the game of living.

We are as young as our self-confidence,

as old as our fear,

as young as our desire,

as old as our despair.

Youth is not a time of life; it is a state of mind.

"I'M MOVING"

EMOTIONAL ISSUES

3
Making A House A Home

- ▲ enough rooms
- ▲ enough square feet
- ▲ a good room layout
- ▲ storage space
- ▲ garage, basement, attic
- ▲ nice neighbors
- ▲ in good condition (not needing maintenance or repair soon)
- ▲ a desirable neighborhood
- ▲ a good lot with attractive landscaping
- ▲ a great view
- ▲ a southern exposure for sunlight

All of these criteria are important to a different extent for different people.

What is it that makes a house a home?

Importantly, it's the people, the relationships and the love. If four members of a family are constantly fighting and in a state of dysfunction, a very important part of the home is lost. "Home is where the heart is" and "Home Sweet Home" are examples of old expressions, which emphasize the human emotions which help make a house a home.

On another level, furnishings help to give hominess to a house.

> I don't know what your destiny will be, but one thing I know, the only ones among you who will be really happy are those who will have sought and found how to serve.
> *Dr. Albert Schweitzer*

23

"I'M MOVING"

> What is it that makes a house a home? Most importantly, it's the people, the relationships and the love.

Attractive furnishings can add a lot of character and warmth to a home. If you love antiques, a house that is filled with antiques will lead you to conclude that it is a beautiful home. Attractive colors to one individual can be very unattractive to others. Furnishings and decorations are a way to personalize a house to make it comfortable as your home.

A white picket fence and a garden are essential in some people's definition of a comfortable home.

Visualizing yourself in the home you desire is essential; moving into a house with the potential to become the home of your dreams is a first step.

A loving atmosphere and your personal furnishings go a long way to developing your concept of a home you want to live in and enjoy for many years.

Have you ever experienced what a divorce can do to a home? The walls, floor and furnishings aren't changed necessarily, but the gestalt, the atmosphere, the loving environment are gone. The house actually has ghosts from the past in the memories of the occupants. It has lost its hominess for the family of the divorce.

Throughout this book we use the word home. This chapter

24

uses the word house as well as home. It had to be said, but from now on only the word "home" will be used to help convey a stronger image of our place to live with PEACE-OF-MIND.

Children are not a part of everyone's life; but they are very important to others.

The Gift of Little Children

They cry at their birth and we are happy,

their lungs work and life outside the

womb has begun.

They long for the touch of their mom and dad,

touching feels good to their nervous

system and their sense of safety and security.

They respond to the voices of their mom and dad,

sounds intrigue them and familiar soothing

sounds of loving voices are the best kind.

They try to see what is around them and

"I'M MOVING"

what they see often delights them

until a smile comes to their lips.

They taste and chew everything in sight to develop

their taste sensation for hard and

soft, yummy and yuck.

They smell without even realizing that

they do; many believe they particularly

know the odor of their mom and dad.

They laugh, they cry, they frown, they

smile, they giggle, they scream,

they yell and they yawn.

And as they grow, they learn and learn

and learn. They learn what is

hot and what is cold.

And as they walk and talk, they

are so pleased. They've begun to

appreciate freedom to move

EMOTIONAL ISSUES

around their surroundings.

How quickly they learn to read a

book and catch

a ball, and throw a toy and

run away fast at bedtime.

How wondrous are the

adventures of learning

to them as they climb and run

and experiment and fall.

And through it all, they yearn so

much for safety, nurturing, hugging, kisses and love.

And as we reflect on the life of a little

child, we as adults

yearn for the very

same things – to love and be loved.

"I'M MOVING"

EMOTIONAL ISSUES

4
Coping With The Emotions Of Moving

Moving usually is connected to some other life experience, which can add anxiety to the move.

> Some men see things as they are and say, "Why?" I dream of things that never were, and say, "Why not?"
> George Bernard Shaw

- Moving to a new city
- Moving to a new job or retirement
- Adding members to the family (like a new baby, or extended family moving in, or a grown child moving back home, etc.)
- Losing members in the family (children grown and left, deaths, family members moved to another state, divorce, an empty nest, etc.)

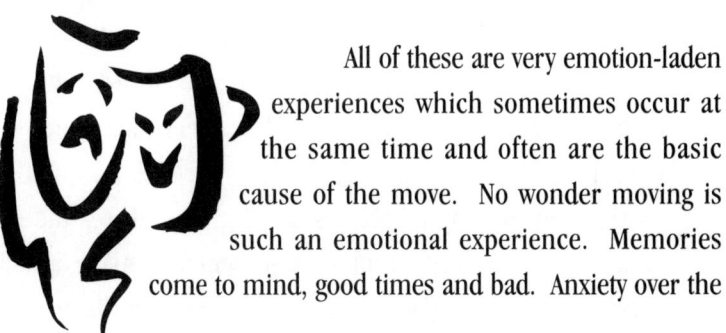

All of these are very emotion-laden experiences which sometimes occur at the same time and often are the basic cause of the move. No wonder moving is such an emotional experience. Memories come to mind, good times and bad. Anxiety over the

29

future is natural. Change and adjustment to new places, new circumstances and new people come hard.

Simple decisions become harder. What grocery store will I shop in? What bank will I use? What doctor or dentist or health plan will I switch to? How can I keep in touch with my old friends? How can I make new friends? What church will I attend? How will I pay the bills? It is no wonder that moving is full of emotions. We need to address our feelings so that they do not engulf our thinking and add untold stress to our body, mind and soul.

It is hard for adults and children to move and handle the stress. Many psychologists say the toughest time emotionally for a child to move is during the teenage years when they are already working so hard to find their identity as a soon-to-be adult, to define their values and confirm them, and to adjust socially with their peers. Children who are ten or under adjust to a move fairly well. Children eleven to seventeen find moving to be a major stress. And, the parents' decision to move can be strongly influenced by the feelings (expressed or unexpressed) of their children.

This leads to the question, "How can the anxiety and stress be reduced or eliminated?" The answer for most people, "Let a professional real estate agent handle most of the details objectively in buying or selling your home." That relieves you of a lot of time which you can apply to your job, your family and your fun in life. Moving can be a pleasant experience with the help of a professional real estate agent who is trained to solve real estate related problems and educate you regarding options.

Consider this scenario: Mary says, "Jack just drives me crazy. Every time we talk, we end up in an argument. He makes me furious." Have you ever experienced this scenario as a first-hand participant? Or as an observer? Or both?

Let's analyze Mary's comments. She is saying that Jack's actions or words have a cause and effect result on her being "crazy" or "furious." That means Jack is directly influencing Mary's emotions – in Mary's view. That makes Mary the victim of Jack's behavior and it happens partly because Mary permits it.

Yes, Mary has some alternatives. Her emotions are hers; they truly come from within her. No one can directly make us happy, sad, angry, furious or crazy. Jack may have certain behavior patterns and use certain words. But only Mary can control Mary's emotions.

PEACE-OF-MIND and good mental health require that we have a filter, which we apply to what we experience, and only after applying the filter do we decide what our emotions will be. **Easier said than done? – absolutely!** But, the filter is critical to our mental health.

My emotions are mine and are valid. No person can make me sad or happy. No person can make me angry or peaceful. Those are my emotional reactions to the stimuli from the world.

I am responsible for all of my own emotions. Therefore, a psychologist or psychiatrist would probably ask Mary to think through why she is letting Jack pull her emotional strings.

We have choices to make in life and one very critical choice is to accept full responsibility for our own emotions. It is a choice for self-empowerment and a choice for PEACE-OF-MIND.

"I'M MOVING"

Goodbye Anxiety

Goodbye anxiety, worry, fear and anger.

Hello trust, love and PEACE-OF-MIND.

Free will is a fabulous gift of choices and

I choose the positive forces of my being.

Anxiety and worry over the possible imagined

outcomes of my life in the future rip

the shreds of my joy in life.

Fear and anger over the events of the past occupy

my mind and spirit in a present

that is entrapped and frozen.

Trust and love, unconditionally, is the

relationship I first seek with everyone

with whom I interact on this earth.

PEACE-OF-MIND will come to those who

choose it over all other alternatives.

Goodbye anxiety, worry, fear and anger.

Hello trust, love and PEACE-OF-MIND.

5
A New Job Opportunity

> One person with courage is a majority.
> *Andrew Johnson*

"We are so happy to tell you that you are being promoted to Manager. You've earned this promotion by your excellent performance in the past three years. You are clearly the top candidate in the company for this great job...in Baltimore."

Pride, more pride...and then the bomb; do my spouse and I really want to move to Baltimore? Of course, in real life it could have been Dallas, Detroit, New York City, Cedar Rapids, Iowa, Geneva, Switzerland or anywhere.

New jobs are exciting, but moving to a new city brings all kinds of fears to our mind and all kinds of questions.

1. What about my spouse and his/her job?
2. What will be the reactions of the children?
3. Can we move in the summer so the children can start school fresh in September?
4. What does a comparable home to ours cost in the new city?
5. How long will we live in the new city before our employer asks us to move again?

6. Is the extra money and job responsibility worth the headaches of moving?
7. Will I get other promotion offers in my present city if I refuse this offer?
8. Will it be difficult to leave all our friends and start making all new ones?
9. Should my promotion be the major consideration, when really this move would affect everyone in the family?
10. Will this new city be closer or further away from our parents and the children's grandparents?

> If the problems expected overshadow the advantages of the move, don't take the promotion and move. If you do decide to move, enjoy it!!

Life's decisions are tough, even when the decision involves supposedly good news of a promotion and more income.

Note: Out of the ten (10) questions which rapidly went through the mind of the person being promoted, only No. 4 involved the home directly. This doesn't mean that question No. 4 was an insignificant one, but ...it is only one of many very important questions.

If you have ever moved to a new city, you could easily add twenty more questions to the list. Moving can be a positive or a negative in our lives.

Some people look at the events of life as Successes or Failures. I personally do not choose to think that way. I have found it much more enjoyable thinking about all of life's events as Successes or Learnings. Thomas Edison tried 1,000 different filaments before he

EMOTIONAL ISSUES

found the best one for a light bulb. That is one success after 999 learnings. Applying this thinking to the promotion to Baltimore…it may be very useful to list the advantages as well as the disadvantages.

- What positive experiences would living in Baltimore offer to us?
- What could we do by living on the East Coast?
- What educational, sports and cultural opportunities would be more available to us?
- How would this change help our family to grow and appreciate the world we live in more?

But there are the realities of finding a new home and selling our present home. Those realities must be faced; here are some tips.

Check with your employer. How will they assist you in selling your home and buying a new home?

- Help with the cost of visiting the new city to shop for a home?
- Help with closing expenses?
- Help with moving expenses?
- Help for your spouse in finding a job in the new city?
- Help with temporary housing expenses in two cities until school is out in June?
- Help with a new mortgage?
- Help if you close on the Baltimore home before your present home is sold?

Your employer wants you to move to the new manager's position in Baltimore. These types of questions will help you and your spouse determine how much the company will help. When interest rates

"I'M MOVING"

were rising dramatically in past years, some companies subsidized part of the mortgage payments at the higher interest rate to entice people to move to a new job in a new city. You need to know what support is available, if any, from your employer. Sometimes just the moving truck bill is $10,000 to $20,000 depending upon how many furnishings you have to move and how far away you are moving.

Find help from real estate agents at both ends. With all the things on your mind, your company will probably encourage you to have a real estate agent to sell your home and another agent to help you buy a new one. It is reasonable to ask your company to help with some or all of the real estate agent commissions.

Don't rush!! This is the time to go a little slowly. Search out three potential real estate brokers and agents to list your present home. Select one after evaluating each of the three marketing plans. Pick an agent and broker you feel has an excellent reputation and references, presents an excellent marketing plan and listens to your needs. In other words, someone you can TRUST to work with you as a team.

On the destination end, you can make your life less anxious by going through the same process – three agents, three plans, and then select the agent you feel you can TRUST.

A good agent will give you PEACE-OF-MIND for all the issues you need to handle.

On top of all the hassles of a new city and a new home, you and your spouse will also be wrestling with new jobs, or even finding a new one in your spouse's case. Moving can be a very stressful time but can be enjoyable by:

a. leaning on the help of real estate agents you can TRUST, and

b. keeping the POSITIVE elements of the move foremost in your mind.

Positive thinking will be a great help in the move. Complaining about how the new city, the new home, the new neighborhood, etc. are not as good as the old will drag you down emotionally.

If the problems expected overshadow the advantages of the move, don't take the promotion and move. The decision for your happiness and your family's happiness is up to you. If you do decide to move, enjoy it!!

Successes and Learnings are good. We can choose not to label anything as Failures. This is a good route to PEACE-OF-MIND.

THE BEST TIME TO BUY AND SELL

6. THE ECONOMY

7. LOCATION, LOCATION, LOCATION

8. A TIME TO SELL AND A TIME TO BUY

9. WIN-WIN NEGOTIATIONS

6
The Economy

> Failure is success
> if we learn from it.
> *Malcolm Forbes*

The Consumer Price Index (CPI) and the Unemployment Rate are often referred to as the key indicators of the health of the economy. If inflation is high, the CPI is high and housing interest rates are usually high. When unemployment is low, the economy is generally providing good job opportunities and consumers are more likely to be in a home-buying mood. The best economic atmosphere occurs when the CPI is low and the unemployment rate is low.

In 1997, the unemployment rate was 4.9%. That was the lowest rate of reported unemployment in twenty-five (25) years: - since 1973. See the following chart:

Year	Unemployment Rate	Year	Unemployment Rate	Year	Unemployment Rate
1970	4.9%	1980	7.1%	1990	5.6%
1971	5.9	1981	7.6	1991	6.8
1972	5.6	1982	9.7	1992	7.5
1973	**4.9**	1983	9.6	1993	6.9
1974	5.6	1984	7.5	1994	6.1
1975	8.5	1985	7.2	1995	5.6
1976	7.7	1986	7.0	1996	5.4
1977	7.1	1987	6.2	**1997**	**4.9**
1978	6.1	1988	5.5		
1979	5.8	1989	5.3		

*Source: U.S. Government – Bureau of Labor Statistics

The consumer's attitude on buying is influenced by the CPI. The CPI measures all costs on an indexed basis. The government estimates that 28% is the average portion of people's incomes that is used for housing, so housing represents 28 % of the government's Consumer Price Index.

Year	CPI	Year	CPI	Year	CPI
1970	5.7%	**1980**	**13.5%**	1990	5.4%
1971	4.4	**1981**	**10.3**	1991	4.2
1972	3.2	1982	6.2	1992	3.0
1973	6.2	1983	3.2	1993	3.0
1974	**11.0**	1984	4.3	1994	2.6
1975	**9.1**	1985	3.6	1995	2.8
1976	5.8	1986	1.9	1996	3.0
1977	6.5	1987	3.6	1997	2.3
1978	7.6	1988	4.1		
1979	**11.3**	1989	4.8		

*Source: U.S. Government – Economic Statistics

In 1997 and 1998 we are enjoying a very low level of the CPI. Consumer confidence is high, unemployment is low, the stock market is strong and everyone agrees we are in a healthy economy.

However, there are times when the CPI is very high and inflation is on everyone's mind. These are times when interest rates on mortgages are generally high and home buying slows dramatically. Two periods in recent history are especially worthy of note. In 1974/1975 the CPI was very high due to rapidly rising oil prices when the oil producing nations dramatically increased crude oil prices. It had a major impact on the CPI and consumer confidence. In 1979, 1980, 1981 the CPI was very high and was one factor which led to Jimmy Carter being defeated by Ronald Reagan for President of the United States in November, 1980. Interest rates on new mortgages on homes went as

The Best Time To Buy And Sell

high as 19%. Lenders were very reluctant to lend except at very high rates. Buyers were very reluctant to borrow at such high rates.

Let's look at the present healthy stock market in relation to history.

U.S. Bear and Bull Stock Markets: N.Y. Stock Exchange
(Source: Frank Cappiello)

Seven Longest Bear Markets Since 1966

Start	End	Approximate Duration (Months)
January 1973	December 1974	23
September 1978	April 1980	19
December 1968	May 1970	17
September 1976	February 1978	17
April 1981	August 1982	16
February 1966	October 1966	8
November 1983	July 1984	8

Seven Longest Bull Markets Since 1966

Start	End	Approximate Duration (Months)
October 1990	Still in progress 6/98	93+
July 1984	August 1987	37
October 1987	July 1990	33
October 1966	December 1968	26
December 1974	September 1976	21
August 1982	November 1983	15
November 1971	January 1973	14

41

"I'M MOVING"

The economy of the country is an important factor to consider. Of course, your personal economic situation is even more important. If a rich uncle leaves you cash at a time when loan interest rates are high and home prices are depressed, you are in an excellent position to buy for cash and get into an attractive home economically. Most of us aren't that fortunate, but the point is that the economy is only part of the equation.

If you have a good income, you can often afford to buy a home even when the economy is weak. In general terms, however, it is very helpful for inflation and unemployment to be low and the stock market to be strong to help the buying public feel good about investing in a home.

"Analyzing The Economy!"

"I'm Moving"

7

Location, Location, Location

> If there's a way to do it better...find it.
>
> *Thomas Edison*

The old expression in real estate is "The three most important criteria in selecting a home are Location, Location and Location." The neighborhood is important to you and important for the resale value of your home.

A second old expression is "Don't buy the most expensive home in the neighborhood." This guidance helps assure that the people who like the neighborhood will be able to buy your home at an attractive price (when you are ready to sell it) to get into their preferred neighborhood.

Of course, you don't just buy a home with resale in mind; you want to enjoy living there. But, resale value is a very important factor to consider. Some areas of the country are zoned very well with clear sections of commercial, farm, resi-

"I'M MOVING"

> Of course, you don't just buy a home with resale in mind; you want to enjoy living there. But, resale value is a very important factor to consider.

dential, and industrial. Some areas are not zoned well and have nice homes, then trailer parks, then a group of car dealers, then nice homes again...all within a very short distance. When you look for a home, it is important to drive around the adjacent sections of town. Even beautiful waterfront property on a lake can have sections with old, small homes, which once were summer cottages...in a general area of beautiful homes on the lake. Of course, over time, the choice land is purchased and the summer cottage is replaced by a more expensive new home. And so it goes – location is very important to your investment decision in a home and to your pleasurable living.

The tables which follow show the median selling prices for homes in different parts of the U.S. (median means just as many homes sold above this price as below it).

Median Home Sales Prices ($ Thousands)
(Basis: 1Q 1998)
(Source: National Association of Realtors)

U.S. Average	**125.9**
Northeast	146.6
Midwest	108.0
South	111.1
West	163.5

The Best Time To Buy And Sell

Selected City Median Sale Price (1Q98)

City	Price	City	Price
Akron, OH	106.2	Lincoln, NE	95.8
Albany, NY	105.4	Los Angeles, CA	176.5
Albequerque, NM	126.2	Louisville, KY	105.7
Amarillo, TX	77.2	Milwaukee, WI	132.2
Anaheim, CA	243.2	Minneapolis/St. Paul, MN	121.9
Appleton, WI	89.1	Nashville, TN	117.6
Atlanta, GA	110.8	New Orleans, LA	96.9
Atlantic City, NJ	110.5	New York Area, NY	178.2
Baltimore, MD	115.5	Oklahoma City, OK	81.2
Baton Rouge, LA	97.1	Orlando, FL	99.3
Beaumont, TX	73.2	Phoenix, AZ	117.3
Birmingham, AL	121.3	Pittsburgh, PA	85.4
Boston, MA	205.2	Portland, ME	94.6
Buffalo, NY	83.2	Portland, OR	155.4
Charlotte, NC	131.8	Providence, RI	119.5
Chicago, IL	161.1	Richmond, VA	118.3
Cleveland, OH	117.0	Saginaw, MI	76.0
Dallas, TX	116.4	Sacramento, CA	116.8
Denver, CO	147.0	St. Louis, MO	95.8
Des Moines, IA	104.0	San Francisco, CA	303.6
Detroit, MI	128.9	Seattle, WA	168.3
El Paso, TX	77.4	Sioux Falls, SD	95.7
Eugene, OR	120.8	Spokane, WA	96.3
Ft. Myers, FL	86.4	Springfield, MA	114.7
Ft. Lauderdale, FL	122.0	Springfield, MO	85.3
Ft. Wayne, IN	87.8	Springfield, IL	85.9
Hartford, CT	134.6	Tampa, FL	84.8
Honolulu, HI	288.5	Topeka, KS	78.4
Houston, TX	92.0	Trenton, NJ	127.2
Kansas City, MO	110.1	Washington, D.C.	163.0
Las Vegas, NV	125.5		

"I'M MOVING"

As an example, Portland, Maine had a median sales price in 1Q 1998 of $94,600 while Portland, Oregon had a median price of $155,400 (64% higher).

The San Francisco Bay Area had a median sale price of $303,600 and Topeka, Kansas had a median sales price of $78,400.

We don't just select our state and city to live in based on the selling price of homes. Where we choose to work in the country plays a major role in where we will live. We may prefer warm weather or cold, near an ocean, near a lake or in the mountains.

No matter how we analyze our decision, location is a very important variable in buying a home – the state, the city and the neighborhood.

Even within a metropolitan area, there are wide differences in the average prices from neighborhood to neighborhood. As an example, the table below shows the average and median selling prices for different neighborhoods in the Minnesota metropolitan area of Minneapolis/St. Paul. Similar information is available in your local community from your Area Association of Realtors®.

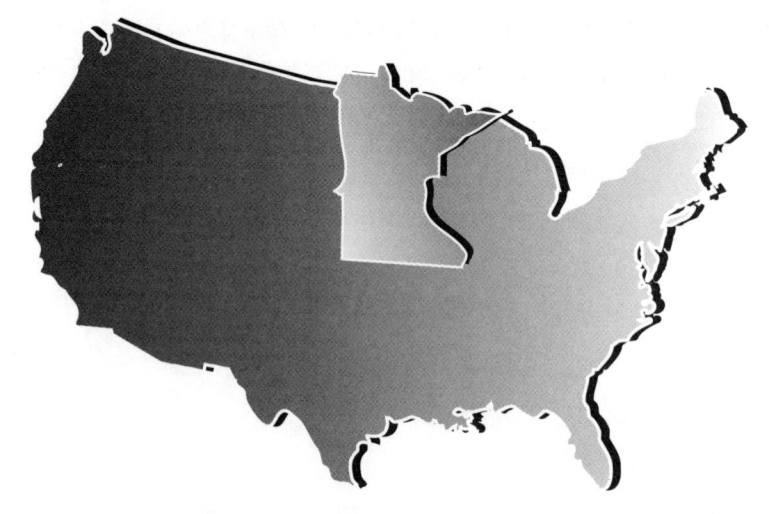

THE BEST TIME TO BUY AND SELL

1997 Home Sales As Reported By
Multiple Listing Service (MLS) Participants

Source: Minneapolis Area Association of Realtors®

District Number and Name		Average Price	Median Price
Division III			
Minneapolis			
300	Calhoun-Isles	$265,775	$200,000
301	Camden	63,175	62,900
302	Central	60,633	59,500
303	Longfellow	87,558	79,900
304	Nokomis	98,608	93,000
305	North	52,102	49,900
306	Northeast	78,892	79,500
307	Phillips	46,790	43,000
308	Powderhorn	65,622	66,000
309	Southwest	154,486	130,900
310	University	101,687	93,000

You can see in #300 Calhoun-Isles that there is a large difference between the average price ($265,775) and the median price ($200,000) because some very expensive homes, which were sold, significantly pulled up the average. In #301 Camden, the average price ($63,175) is extremely close to the median price ($62,900) indicating that there are very few, very high priced homes, which were sold in Camden in 1997.

"I'M MOVING"

District Number and Name		Average Price	Median Price
Suburban and other areas			
340	Buffalo	117,652	109,000
341	Wright County	111,998	109,000
342	Hutchinson	109,355	97,200
343	McLeod County	80,267	77,500
360	Robbinsdale	94,440	90,000
361	Crystal	96,002	91,000
362	New Hope	118,677	119,000
363	Brooklyn Center	88,034	88,500
364	Brooklyn Park	121,679	114,900
365	Maple Grove/Osseo	169,582	143,000
366	Champlin	127,467	116,000
367	Hennepin Co North	165,377	156,900
368	Hennepin Co NW	238,270	180,000
370	Sibley County	93,598	89,500
373	Golden Valley	145,307	132,000
374	Plymouth	210,497	188,500
378	Richfield	105,706	105,900
379	Bloomington-East	109,986	107,000
380	Bloomington-West	173,048	145,500
381	Lake Minnetonka	282,465	186,000
385	Edina	254,207	210,000
386	Hopkins	127,460	111,000
387	Minnetonka	213,273	170,000
391	St. Louis Park	124,672	114,500
392	Eden Prairie	240,666	201,000
394	Carver County	128,675	118,100
395	Waterfront	121,029	109,000
396	Chanhassen	222,315	200,000
397	Chaska	170,366	144,900
398	Victoria	229,112	206,993
399	Out of Town	87,985	75,000

District Number and Name		Average Price	Median Price
Division II			
600	West St. Paul	103,434	94,900
602	South St. Paul	88,615	87,000
604	Mendota-Lilydale-Mendota Hts.	200,839	185,500
605	Sunfish Lake	551,475	830,000
608	Inver Grove Heights	155,743	129,000
610	Eagan	172,306	154,500
612	Burnsville	154,888	137,400
614	Apple Valley	168,141	143,000
616	Rosemount	140,882	128,900
617	Hastings	123,190	112,500
618	Eastern Dakota County	148,814	139,900
624	Farmington	123,819	119,000
626	Lakeville	172,538	153,400
628	Southern Dakota County	137,518	129,000
630	Northfield	140,049	128,900
632	Rice County	104,398	92,000
640	Shakopee	133,925	120,215
642	Prior Lake	184,263	152,500
644	Savage	149,275	137,500
646	Jordan	120,451	116,000
648	New Prague	131,985	119,900
650	Belle Plaine	111,381	113,000
658	LeSueur County	81,965	81,500
660	Goodhue County	105,893	94,000

"I'M MOVING"

District Number and Name		Average Price	Median Price
Division I			
702	Falcon Hts-Lauderdale-Roseville	140,482	123,500
705	Lino Lakes-Hugo-Centerville	149,114	132,691
706	North Central Suburban	217,257	152,000
707	Ham Lake	143,969	130,500
708	White Bear Area	155,386	125,000
709	Forest Lake Area	141,077	128,500
710	Northeast Anoka County	123,075	120,000
711	Southern Chisago county	118,315	111,900
712	Maplewood-North St. Paul	120,569	114,700
713	Bethel	118,081	119,900
714	Phalen	73,770	72,500
716	Hillcrest/Hazel Park/Dayton's Bluff	73,159	75,000
720	Southeast St. Paul	105,884	104,000
721	Lakeland-Afton-Denmark	208,032	177,904
722	Newport-St. Paul Park-Cottage Grove	116,322	111,500
725	Pine Springs-Lake Elmo-Oakdale	145,380	129,000
726	Woodbury	193,212	175,000
727	Stillwater-Bayport	191,459	157,000
728	Riverview-Cherokee	70,414	69,900
738	Home Croft-W 7th	67,980	68,900
740	Crocus Hill	191,201	166,500
742	Central	57,943	58,750
744	Como	98,812	96,900
746	St. Anthony-Midway	92,680	79,200
748	Town & Country-Merriam Park	135,653	119,900

MORE EMOTIONAL ISSUES

District Number and Name		Average Price	Median Price
750	Mac-Groveland-River Road Area	139,499	123,000
752	Highland Area	148,822	128,000
754	Big Lake Township	108,190	104,500
756	Elk River	126,417	119,900
758	Northwestern Anoka County	125,555	117,500
760	Ramsey	131,242	120,920
762	Andover	141,699	129,900
764	Blaine	119,159	113,000
765	Arden Hills-Shoreview	172,850	148,000
766	Mndsvw-New Brgtn-St. Anth. Vill.	126,378	118,900
767	Coon Rapids	113,891	107,500
768	Fridley	106,308	98,900
769	Anoka	104,258	99,900
770	Hilltop-Columbia Heights	86,079	84,500
771	Spring Lake Park	96,736	96,281
772	Lexington-Circle Pines	111,676	108,000
780	Sherburne County	104,357	97,800
782	Isanti County	106,410	99,500
783	Cambridge	92,115	90,000
784	Northern Chisago County	83,824	81,900
795	Waterfront	99,536	84,500
798	Out of Town	76,735	73,500
805	Western Wisconsin	114,376	105,000

Back to the original premise of Location, Location, Location. Knowing the neighborhoods in your community is very helpful in real estate and it is very important to have a knowledgeable real estate advisor working for you. When you learn about the neighborhoods, average prices, median prices, zoning laws, schools, parks, lakes, etc., you become a much smarter home buyer.

8
A Time To Sell And A Time To Buy

The History of Mortgage Interest Rates

When a buyer has the desire to purchase a home, an important question then becomes, "What are the interest rates on a mortgage and what will be my down payment?"

Note in Table I that interest rates didn't vary much over a 40-year period (1920 to 1959) even though we went through the Great Depression, World War II and the Korean War in that period. The lowest annual interest rate on a mortgage during the 40-year period was 4.70% in 1945, the last year of World War II. The highest year (1921) averaged 5.97%.

> It is one of the most beautiful compensations of this life that no man can sincerely try to help another without helping himself.
>
> *Ralph Waldo Emerson*

55

Table I
Mortgage Interest Rates
(30-year, fixed rate, conventional mortgages)
Source: Annual Statistical Digest/Federal Reserve Bulletin

Year	Interest %	Year	Interest %
1920	5.75	1940	5.03
1921	**5.97**	1941	4.90
1922	5.95	1942	4.98
1923	5.91	1943	4.77
1924	5.92	1944	4.71
1925	5.90	**1945**	**4.70**
1926	5.89	1946	4.74
1927	5.88	1947	4.80
1928	5.85	1948	4.91
1929	5.92	1949	4.93
1930	5.95	1950	4.95
1931	5.75	1951	4.93
1932	5.77	1952	5.03
1933	5.60	1953	5.09
1934	5.45	1954	5.15
1935	5.26	1955	5.18
1936	5.09	1956	5.19
1937	5.11	1957	5.42
1938	5.00	1958	5.58
1939	5.05	1959	5.71

Mortgage interest rates exceeded 11% in the seven (7) year period 1979 to 1985 as shown in Table II. With that perspective of history, the rates in 1997 and to date in 1998 have been very attractive.

Table II
Mortgage Interest Rates
(30-year, fixed rate, conventional mortgages)
Source: Annual Statistical Digest/Federal Reserve Bulletin

Year	Interest %	Year	Interest %
1960	6.30	**1980**	**13.95**
1961	6.97	**1981**	**14.74**
1962	5.93	**1982**	**15.12**
1963	5.81	**1983**	**12.66**
1964	5.80	**1984**	**12.37**
1965	5.83	**1985**	**11.90**
1966	6.40	1986	10.39
1967	6.53	1987	10.40
1968	7.12	1988	10.38
1969	7.99	1989	10.26
1970	8.56	1990	10.01
1971	7.74	1991	9.09
1972	7.70	1992	8.27
1973	8.33	1993	7.17
1974	9.23	1994	8.28
1975	9.14	1995	7.86
1976	9.04	1996	7.76
1977	9.00	**1997**	**7.73**
1978	9.70	**1998**	**7.14**
1979	**11.16**		(As of July 1998)

You can see that interest rates are relatively attractive in 1998. Four (4) consecutive years below 8% last occurred in the late 1960's...about 30 years ago. The late 1990's is a very attractive interest rate market. And, with the Consumer Price Index low and the

Unemployment Rate low, it is an especially attractive real estate market for buyers and for sellers. The economy and the stock market are both very strong. The Conference Board, which measures consumer confidence across the U.S. monthly, reported that June 1998 recorded the highest level of consumer confidence in the past 29 years. It is not surprising that Mid-1998, as this book goes to press, is a hot real estate sales period.

In the very high interest rate period of 1980 to 1982, when individual conventional mortgage rates often were over 15%, other mortgages such as FHA and VA mortgages with very low down payment requirements, were only available at 17 to 19%. Lenders were requiring high interest rates and borrowers were resisting purchasing a home with the resultant high monthly payments.

Although almost everyone prefers low inflation, low interest rates and low unemployment, it is not to be expected to continue long term – based on history.

When the economy is healthy, it is generally a good time to sell (because there are many willing buyers) and also a good time to buy (because interest rates are attractive).

Axioms

1. Good economic times lead to good real estate appreciation.
2. If possible, sell your home when economic conditions in the country are generally good. Buy, if possible, when the economy is weak.

9
Win-Win Negotiations

The home we buy or sell will be valued in dollars in the final transaction. Our thoughts may lead us to get the best price on the sale of our home so that we have the most dollars to invest in another home or other investments.

> Whether you think you can or think you can't – you are right.
>
> Henry Ford

We often think of negotiation as a process where the person with the most information or the most leverage wins. Is there always a winner and a loser? I suggest that there are winners and losers only if we choose to think that way.

We are all accustomed to WIN-LOSE negotiations in the transactions of our lives. The transactions are staged like military battles, us versus the enemy, good versus evil, and we always want to win.

The sports analogy is heard often, tactics to use to deceive the other party to the transaction, so your team wins. Pick the best players for your team, so you can win. Even establishing the rules of the game to your advantage is commonly thought to be a good negotiation technique.

> An attitude of Win-Win negotiations is the most positive way to achieve PEACE-OF-MIND and eliminate anxiety.

Well times are changing!! The prestigious Harvard Law School has been teaching WIN-WIN negotiation techniques for fifteen (15) years. And, the experienced negotiators of the business world are moving in that direction.

PEACE-OF-MIND results from WIN-WIN negotiations: that's probably the most important reason to avoid WIN-LOSE tactics.

Let's analyze a transaction of the buying and selling of a home. At the final closing, both the buyer and the seller sign papers and exchange money indicating that they are pleased with the terms of the transaction. That certainly could be called a Win-Win result. The seller accomplished the objective of selling in a reasonable amount of time for a good price. The buyer accomplished the objective of purchasing the home for a fair price.

If the final closing can be Win-Win, then we just need to find ways to have an attitude of Win-Win throughout the entire process so that we can go through the buying or selling with PEACE-OF-MIND.

The customized market analysis prepared for you by your real estate advisor is a valuable resource because it shows you as a buyer the sold price of comparable homes and the asking price for those still on the market. This is the same information, which the seller's agent provides to the seller.

The negotiation, with the help of your real estate agent, will have a great deal of the anxiety eliminated, if both buyer and seller are looking at similar lists of competitively comparable properties. Your agent will be providing a valuable service by providing this information very early in your discussions. In fact, a good customized market analysis should be one of the important reasons for you to choose your real estate agent in the first place.

When do negotiations seem to become Win-Lose? Both sides are asking the question, "What's in it for me?" or "How can I make the other person a loser?" Each side has key needs and wants. Price is an important variable to both buyer and seller. But often there are many other variables to be negotiated. The buyer may want to include the refrigerator and the dining room chandelier and the seller may want to take those with them to their new home. The buyer may want to obtain certain financing that requires the seller to pay one point (1% of the mortgage loan). Each of these items needs to be discussed to reach a successful closing. Once you have decided that you have a reasonably good offer from a buyer – you will want to calmly analyze your alternatives with your agent. Whether you are the seller or the buyer, you can greatly benefit by extensive discussions on negotiation strategy with your agent. If one person gets stubborn and insists on their point of view or is not objective, with no compromise, the sales transaction can fall apart completely. That happens when one party is negotiating in a Win-Lose atmosphere. For example, the home is listed for $120,000 after an extensive competitive market analysis is completed. Experience shows that the final selling price often averages about 3% below the listing price, but this depends on the economy and the current market. Now, a buyer submits a purchase agreement for $105,000. The seller is upset and may counter with $119,000, not choosing to negotiate seriously with such a low initial offer. "Low ball" offers often are unproductive when the seller has many alternatives. After the house has been on the market for 90 or 120 days without selling, the $105,000 offer may be more interesting to the sellers. Even though they would like a higher price, they've learned from experience that their $120,000 listing price wasn't attracting buyers. They may choose to reduce their listing price, change to a new listing agent or both.

An attitude of Win-Win negotiations is the most positive way to achieve PEACE-OF-MIND and eliminate anxiety. Visualize a successful closing with everyones' objectives being satisfactorily met (timing, dollars, etc.). Visualize everyone satisfied at the closing table and wishing each other luck for the future. Visualize good will and friendly handshakes. If you can come close to your original goals with PEACE-OF-MIND, you can be very pleased.

The expression, "What goes around, comes around" is a version of the Golden Rule – "Do unto others as you would have others do unto you." Win-Win negotiations are a matter of attitude. With help from a professional real estate advisor, you will most likely have an enjoyable as well as successful transaction.

SELECTING AN AGENT

10. SUGGESTIONS ON SELECTING SOMEONE TO MARKET YOUR HOME

11. THE REAL ESTATE BROKER AND THE REAL ESTATE AGENT

12. TIPS FOR THE BUYER

13. YOUR TIME IS VALUABLE

14. FORMS, FORMS, AND MORE FORMS

15. YOUR COMFORTABLE HOME IS PROBABLY NOT READY TO SELL

10

Suggestions On Selecting Someone To Market Your Home

> Honesty is the first chapter of the book of wisdom.
>
> *Thomas Jefferson*

Let's face it, there are excellent golfers and there are duffers. There are excellent carpenters and there are carpenters you would not want to build even a shed for you. Yes, there are excellent real estate agents and very poor ones. How can you find an excellent one?

Here are some simple tips to help you select a realtor.

1. Ask around. Were you happy with the agent you used before? Do you have some friends who are real estate agents? Have some of your friends moved and told you they were pleased with their agents?
2. What real estate companies in your community have a good reputation? Which are the largest? What have you heard about some smaller companies with an office very close to you?

By this process, you will be able to identify three agents and/or three brokers. You may be impatient and decide to work with the first real estate sales agent you meet who seems quite pleasant and knowledgeable. However, to make yourself feel very comfortable with your choice, you may want to interview two, or we would suggest three. After three interviews you will feel very good about the one you select. If you only want to interview two, that is better than just one. If you are going with just one, we urge you to either have had great first-hand experience with them or an extremely strong recommendation from a very close friend of yours.

Whether you decide to talk to one, two or three, you should ask them to provide you with a comprehensive marketing plan BEFORE YOU SIGN TO LIST YOUR HOME WITH THEM.

You will recognize a good marketing plan when you see one. A good plan answers these questions:

1. How will you be kept informed about appointments for people coming into your home?
2. When will you hear feedback on the results of the showings from your agent?
3. When will Open Houses occur and how will they be promoted?
4. Who is the target market?
5. What advertising will be done on your home, in what publications and in what frequency?
6. Is a thorough analysis completed of comparable properties that are on the market now or recently sold? This needs to be done so that you can select a reasonable listing price.

When you sign a listing agreement, most real estate companies will be asking you to have them as your exclusive sales representative for three to six months. On very expensive homes that have a limited number of potential buyers, they may ask for as much as twelve months. There are ways to include the terms of cancellation into a listing agreement, but both the seller and the sales agent you enter into the agreement with should have a common goal – to work together in good faith to sell the home for the best possible price in a reasonable amount of time.

Homes which are listed at competitive prices, sell in the shortest amount of time; that's reasonable. Your agent needs to do a very thorough analysis so that you feel comfortable in establishing the listing price. Yes, that's your responsibility, so you want a very good analysis giving you confidence that you are not too high or too low on the listing price. Too high will lead buyers to seek other homes and you will be a lot longer selling your home. Too low, and you are losing money.

Review of the marketing plan from one, two or three potential real estate agents will give you a good feeling about the competence of the agent and company to represent your interests. With this approach, when you sign the listing agreement, you also have in your hand the promised marketing plan, which is the responsibility of your agent and his broker to perform. It is their job to expose your home to the market and generate activity. The agent who listed your home often is not the person who sells it.

The result, most likely, will be a happy ending – your home sold at a competitive price in a reasonable amount of time with few hassles.

Suppose you have a 90-day agreement and you are unhappy with your sales agent or the results, or both. Now, it is time to consider a new agent. Perhaps the agent who was second best in your interviewing of three, would be a candidate. Or, an agent who showed your property several times.

However you think about it, reviewing the marketing plans from several real estate agents is generally wise BEFORE YOU SIGN A LISTING AGREEMENT.

"I'm Moving"

11

The Real Estate Broker And The Real Estate Agent

Summary

1. The seller employs a real estate broker to list the home for sale. The sales agent of the broker works out the details for the seller and is called the real estate agent.

2. For example, Mrs. Smith employs Broker ABC to list her home for sale. The details are handled by real estate agent Robinson.

> The greatest mistake a person can make is to be afraid of making one.
> *Elbert Hubbard*

```
              Listing For Sale
 ┌────────┐   ┌──────────────┐   ┌────────┐
 │ Seller │──▶│ Real Estate  │──▶│ Broker │
 │ Smith  │   │Agent Robinson│   │  ABC   │
 └────────┘   └──────────────┘   └────────┘
```

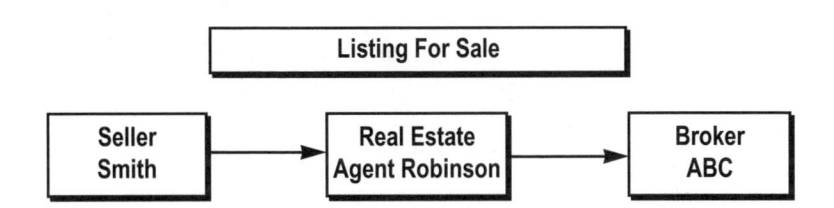

3. Broker ABC arranges for all of its listings (homes for sale) to be posted in the MLS (Multiple Listing Service). Broker ABC generally employs many sales agents.

4. Agent Robinson arranges for open house showings and advertising of the home for sale – including the sign in the front yard which has Broker ABC's and real estate agent Robinson's names and phone numbers prominently displayed.
5. Buyers can contact real estate agent Robinson directly if they choose (e.g., at an open house or by phone).
6. Often, a potential buyer wants a real estate agent of his choice to help him find a suitable home to buy.
7. As an example, Buyer Brown employs real estate agent Johnson to represent him, search the market and show Buyer Brown the homes which best meet Buyer Brown's criteria (neighborhood, size of home, price of home, etc.). Johnson is a sales agent for Broker XYZ.

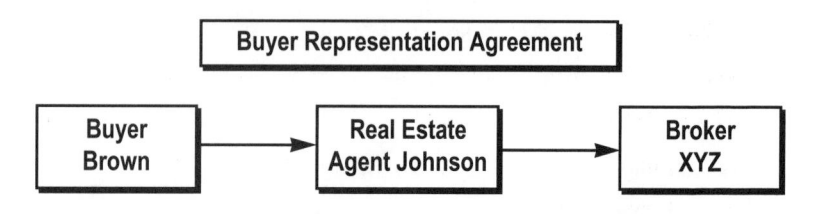

```
          Buyer Representation Agreement
  Buyer           Real Estate           Broker
  Brown    →     Agent Johnson    →      XYZ
```

8. Real estate agent Johnson helps Buyer Brown in the search for a home and also helps him with the negotiations.

   Agent Robinson, as we discussed earlier, helps Seller Smith in promoting her home for sale and also helps her with the negotiations.
9. At the closing, Buyer Brown provides the money to Broker XYZ. Broker XYZ provides the money to Broker ABC and then Broker ABC provides the money to Seller Smith (less appropriate closing costs and commissions – all of which are explained well before closing). A negotiated commission is paid by Seller Smith to Listing Broker ABC and is divided among the brokers, the selling agent and the listing agent.

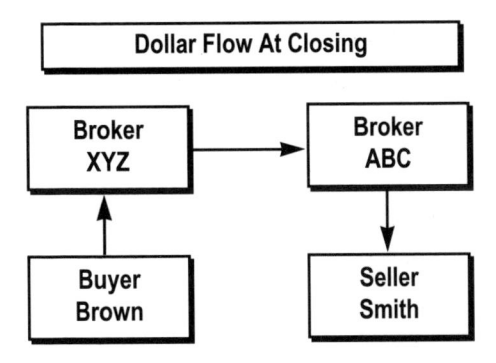

```
         ┌─────────────────────────┐
         │   Dollar Flow At Closing │
         └─────────────────────────┘

     ┌──────────┐         ┌──────────┐
     │  Broker  │────────▶│  Broker  │
     │   XYZ    │         │   ABC    │
     └──────────┘         └──────────┘
           ▲                    │
           │                    ▼
     ┌──────────┐         ┌──────────┐
     │  Buyer   │         │  Seller  │
     │  Brown   │         │  Smith   │
     └──────────┘         └──────────┘
```

10. When buyers and sellers decide that they prefer to handle the details themselves and absorb the risks and anxieties in this field where they are not knowledgeable professionals, they do so via "For Sale By Owner." The reward can be the savings of sales commissions. The downside can be many strangers visiting your home who are not qualified to buy, legal problems, time delay problems, unsuccessful negotiations, and long-term problems with the purchase or sale, which professional real estate agents would have resolved. Also, buyers often want to deduct the sales commissions saved from their offer.

11. For the protection of sellers and buyers, the sales agents are required to very fully inform their clients in writing, with signatures.

12. The simplified case described is not the only approach, but it is by far the most common scenario.

"I'm Moving"

"A salesman? I don't have time to listen to a salesman, we have a battle to fight!"

12
Tips For The Buyer

> I am imagination.
> I can see what the eyes cannot see. I can hear what the ears cannot hear. I can feel what the heart cannot feel.
>
> *Peter Nivio Zarlenga*

Once you have decided that buying a home is a good idea, you should think about a plan for buying.

Sure, there are circumstances which don't require a plan. "The lease for your apartment is complete in two months. You just got a nice job promotion and salary increase. Your cousin has to leave town quickly to move to California and you have a great opportunity to buy your cousin's home, which you absolutely love, at a very attractive price."

Getting back to more normal situations, a plan for buying is generally a good idea.

Phase I:

As you drive around neighborhoods that you like and see a "For Sale" sign, call the number on the sign and get the asking price for the home. You are only seeing the home from the outside, but you can start developing an understanding of the market prices compared to your needs and wants. (Note: You can get an agent involved at any phase where you want the help.)

Phase II:

Attending a few "Open House" showings is a good idea to help you get a rough understanding of the market and how much the market price is for a home about the size you are considering in the neighborhood you are considering. This will be a reality check to give you an idea of how much house is selling for how many dollars. You can get confused by seeing too many "Open Houses", but 2 to 4 will give you some perspective at this stage.

Phase III:

Now, you may find it is good to confirm your buying power, or more appropriately – your borrowing power. Chapter 16, "What price home can I qualify for?," goes into some detail on this step.

Phase IV:

With a rough understanding of the market, your needs and your buying power, you now want to select a real estate agent to help you. You can do it yourself, but not with the PEACE-OF-MIND this book is suggesting may be very important to you. A real estate agent is a professional in the area where you now can benefit by professional help because you have done some homework (Phases I, II, and III).

The most important quality you are looking for in a real estate agent is TRUST. You want to be able to TRUST your agent to work hard on your behalf, to be very knowledgeable about the market, to listen carefully to your needs, to provide you with information and creative alternatives, and to always keep their promises. When an agent whom you are considering hiring promises to meet you at 2:00 p.m. and by 3:00 p.m. hasn't called and then rushes up to your door, you are beginning to wonder if she will keep her promises.

If you are ready to buy, you may want to interview several agents. Of course, if you already have had a good experience with an agent, he/she may be right for you again. Some agents, however, are specialists in different types of homes and particular neighborhoods or prefer to represent sellers rather than buyers.

When you are interviewing agents to help you buy a home, remember you are hiring them. You want to TRUST them and feel comfortable working with them. If you have reservations about an agent, that probably is a good signal to work with someone else in whom you have more confidence. **You want unquestionable honesty in your agent.**

> You want to be able to TRUST your agent to work hard on your behalf, to be very knowledgeable about the market, to listen carefully to your needs, to provide you with information and creative alternatives, and to always keep their promises.

The agent will have to be a good listener to understand your needs and wants. You want someone who knows the communities you are interested in and is experienced in negotiations. The agent should work with a reputable broker who is also part of the Multiple Listing Service (MLS) so that your agent can readily search by computer for all the available homes for sale from all companies who participate in the MLS.

A good agent will take your needs and wants, compare them to the total market availability and together you both will select good home candidates. Then, the agent will make appointments and take you to tour the homes you

"I'M MOVING"

want to see. When you are ready to place a purchase offer on a given home, your agent will be your negotiator. You always make the decision, $1,000 more, $1,000 less, whatever – but the agent and you can discuss negotiation strategies before you make the decision. Here again, that's why you want full TRUST and confidence in your real estate agent.

Selecting an agent can be enjoyable if you remind yourself that you and your agent are a team. Once you have selected an agent and toured homes with them, you may have made a friend for life. Buying a home should be a pleasurable experience: PEACE-OF-MIND as you go through the process, Closing and a Good Outcome (That's the Phase V goal).

Establishing Feasibility (on your own or with an agent)

Phase I	Phase II	Phase III

Selecting an Agent and Analyzing Candidate Homes

Phase IV

PEACE-OF-MIND

Closing And A Good Outcome

Phase V

Trust

To trust is to bond with another person

with great confidence and pleasure.

A person you can trust knows that they can trust you

and your word to be honest and fair.

Trust is a mutual respect and allegiance

based on sincere good will.

We are cautious whom we trust and it is healthy

to test boundaries to avoid being hurt.

When we have found someone to not have been trustworthy,

we may take quite a while to trust them again.

Trust must be earned through

consistency and predictability.

A bond of friendship is to be treasured

when it includes a bond of unconditional trust.

Those we can trust are those who we want to spend time with

and who make us feel good about ourselves.

"I'M MOVING"

13
Your Time Is Valuable

> Courage is resistance to fear, mastery of fear – not the absence of fear.
> *Mark Twain*

Perhaps you want to use your valuable time for your work, family, recreational activities, charity activities or for anything important to you. Time is limited, we even need a good night's sleep and time for a walk and to relax.

So, do you want to use your time to learn what a real estate agent knows? Probably not.

What does the real estate agent do for you to help you have time for yourself – and PEACE-OF-MIND on the sale or purchase of your home?

- Listens and understands your real estate needs.
- Finds a buyer for your home or finds a home for you by doing all the market analysis, advertising and reviewing customized opportunities with you.
- Helps you determine the price home for which you can qualify.
- Connects you with a mortgage company should you desire.
- Connects you with a title insurance company at your request, which usually conducts the closing.

"I'M MOVING"

- Provides information and contacts on home inspection companies.
- Provides information and contacts on home insurance companies.
- Represents you in all negotiations.

Note, to define the relationships between you, the real estate sales agent and the sales agent's broker, a written agreement is wise to clearly define everyone's responsibilities. For your protection, you should insist that your agreement with your real estate sales agent be made in writing in plain English. That is the business-like way to proceed.

We learn more by listening than we do by talking.

Even honest people can disagree several months from the time a discussion was held as to the specifics. You should politely, but firmly, ask that your relationship with your real estate sales agent be in writing and signed by both parties. A professional real estate agent will also prefer a written mutual understanding. All of your questions should be addressed in the agreement.

Free Customized Market Analysis

When you are considering the sale of your home, a frequent question in your mind is, "What is a fair selling price which will permit me to sell in a relatively short amount of time?"

If you wanted to know the current price of various refrigerators, you

Selecting An Agent

would check the market in various stores for new refrigerators of different models and check the classified ads for used refrigerators. Similarly, if you wanted to analyze the prices for new and used cars, you would check with auto dealers for new cars, and with dealers and individuals (via classifieds) for used cars.

A real estate agent has access to all of that type information for homes similar, but probably not identical, to yours. Some homes sold in the last six months to a year were like yours in size, amenities and neighborhood. Some are on the market right now. Location and neighborhood are extremely important factors in predicting real estate value.

A market analysis is as thorough as the real estate agent who does it. A very careful analysis will give you a very good idea of a fair selling price. The more information you provide to your agent and the more analysis the agent provides, the closer the report will be to a "customized" market analysis. The homes used for comparison will be the type of homes which a buyer would most likely consider before purchasing your home.

> You should politely, but firmly, ask that your relationship with your real estate sales agent be in writing and signed by both parties. A professional real estate agent will also prefer a written mutual understanding.

Most real estate agents are pleased to provide this analysis for you free of charge so it is a good option to consider to add to your knowledge base *before you pick the final real estate agent to sell your home.*

"I'M MOVING"

14
Forms, Forms, And More Forms

> It's what you learn after you know it all that counts.
> John Wooden

Buying or selling a home is not simple legally. The State and Federal governments have set a lot of rules to help document all of the particulars in all real estate transactions so that the consumer is fully informed. However, these useful consumer protection efforts lead to a lot of forms in a transaction.

As an example, on the next page is a listing of the Minnesota possible forms; most of the applicable forms need to be signed to be valid. "Required" and "possible" forms may be different in each state.

This list of forms can be a headache for the average buyer or seller unless she is utilizing a professional real estate agent. Working together, PEACE-OF-MIND is the goal.

- Real Estate Transfer Disclosure Form
- Listing Agreement
- Sellers Property Disclosure Agreement
- Buyer Representation Agreement
- Buyer Information Sheet or Lender Letter
- Purchase Agreement
- Personal Property Agreement
- Cancellation of Listing Agreement
- Cancellation of Buyer Representation Agreement
- Financing Addendum – FHA Insured Mortgage
- Financing Addendum – VA Guaranteed Mortgage
- Financing Addendum – Conventional or Privately Insured Conventional Mortgage
- Financing Addendum – Contract for Deed
- Financing Addendum Assumption
- Lenders Mortgage Rate Lock – In Document
- Appraisal Report
- Home Inspection Report
- Buyer Purchasing "As Is" Addendum
- Closing Information Sheet
- Well Disclosure Statement
- Private Sewer System and/or Well Location Map
- Private Sewer System Disclosure
- Condominium/Townhouse/Cooperative Addendum
- Addendum to Purchase Agreement Disclosure of Information on Lead-Based Paint and Lead-Based Paint Hazards
- Contingency Addendum
- Request for Removal of Contingency
- Inspection Contingency Addendum
- Amendment to Purchase Agreement – Seller Holdover Possession Agreement "Rent Back"
- Vacant Land Addendum

15

Your Comfortable Home Is Probably Not Ready To Sell

The goals of a seller are:
- to receive a fair price for their home,
- in a short period of time,
- with minimum hassles.

> You will become as small as your controlling desire; as great as your dominant aspiration.
>
> *James Allen*

Put yourself in the mindset of potential buyers. They have normal human emotions; they make quick initial judgments. First impressions may not be accurate, but all buyers react strongly to their first impressions.

A great first impression and they are willing to look further. A bad first impression and they are turned off and tuned out.

So, let's make a short list of what may be "comfortable" to the homeowner and yet would "turn off" many buyers. The recommended actions to be taken to make the home more attractive to buyers are also noted. There are no rules, but generally you can expect to sell quicker and for a better price if you follow the recommended actions.

Comfortable for the owner

We have four children and we want our home to be comfortable for them. The children's bicycles and toys are often on the front lawn in the summer. We don't always get to the lawn mowing on a rigid schedule. We have many items on our "to do" list but pruning the bushes and weeding are not high on the list. We need to paint the front door but haven't gotten to it.

- Turn-off for many buyers

Initial impression, curb appeal (when the buyer is sitting in a car and just looking at the home), is bad. "Clutter, poor landscaping, just make me feel the inside of the home also probably isn't taken care of. Let's skip this home and go on to the next one on our list," says a typical buyer.

- **Recommended Actions**

    Pay attention to the initial outside appearance. Paint, pick up and minor trimming don't take much time or money. They are very important to the first impression in selling a home.

Comfortable for the owner

We want our children to be able to express their full personalities so they each get to pick the paint color and carpeting for their room. Their posters are their choice.

- Turn off for many buyers

"I can't visualize my furniture in this home. Nothing will go with a dark blue wall and stars on the ceiling. Nothing will go with green bathroom tile. The home looks so cluttered and dark. Let's go on to another home."

- **Recommended Actions**

  Buyers need a setting which is compatible with their lifestyle and furnishings. The best choices to appeal to buyers are:
  - *Paint with neutral colors throughout the home.*
  - *Take down all posters.*
  - *Move out any extra furniture or "stuff" (then the house looks larger to a potential buyer).*
  - *Paint and pick up; which doesn't cost much money (the green tile may be okay to someone – don't redo the tile just for selling your home – that's too much money to spend).*
  - *Put on every light in the home when it is being shown to a potential buyer. People like homes tidy, bright, light and clean.*

> When you are selling, the home should look tidy, bright, light and clean. The payoff in dollars and a fast sale is worth the effort.

Comfortable for the owner

I'd like to talk to the people who are interested in buying our home. We've lived here for 20 years and I can tell them about the neighborhood, the park, the condition of our roof, our great playroom that we remodeled downstairs, etc. Also, our dog is very friendly and a new buyer will be

"I'M MOVING"

pleased to see the flap in the garage door where the dog can come in and out on its own.

- Turn off for many buyers

"If there are family members in the home, I'll just avoid seeing those rooms. I don't want to be rude and intrude on them. Also, I don't want to insult them by making some comment they can hear that is negative about their home."

> - **Recommended Actions**
>   - *No family members, at all, in the home while it is being shown by a real estate agent to a prospective buyer.*
>   - *No pets on the premises – okay, maybe goldfish – but no cats, dogs, etc.*

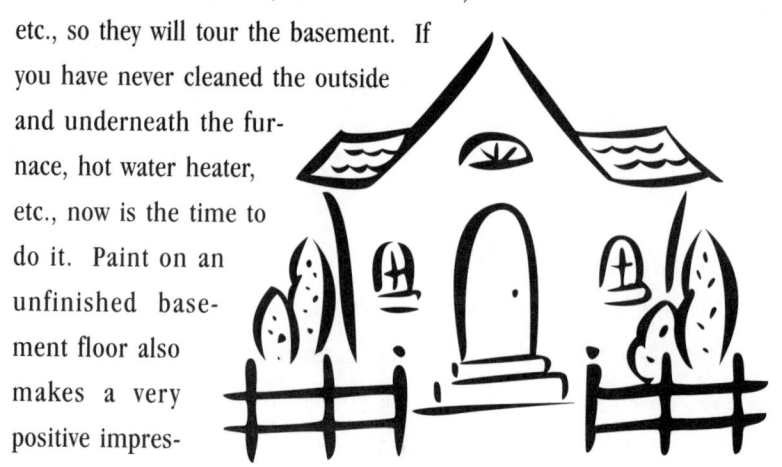

These three simple scenarios will give you the general idea about preparing your home for sale. As you can imagine, you don't want a large van parked in the driveway. The garage is best to have no cars in it, but yet it looks orderly. The basement is clean, orderly and brightly lit. Yes, people want to see the furnace, hot water heater, etc., so they will tour the basement. If you have never cleaned the outside and underneath the furnace, hot water heater, etc., now is the time to do it. Paint on an unfinished basement floor also makes a very positive impression to a buyer.

The key is to put yourself in the mindset of the variety of buyers who will tour your home. The goal is to have them visualize themselves, their family and their furnishings in the home. If the potential negatives are not in sight, they can better visualize themselves in the home.

After the new buyers move in, they will undoubtedly become "comfortable" with their own clutter, their own colors, etc. But, it is important when you are selling; the home should look tidy, bright, light and clean. The payoff in dollars and a fast sale is worth the effort.

"I'M MOVING"

FINANCIAL ISSUES

16. WHAT PRICE HOME CAN I QUALIFY FOR?
17. MORTGAGES AND MONTHLY PAYMENTS
18. SHOPPING FOR A MORTGAGE
19. SALES COMMISSIONS
20. ROGER'S REMODELING ADVENTURE
21. THE TITLE AND TITLE INSURANCE
22. THE WISDOM OF A HOME INSPECTION

FINANCIAL ISSUES

16
What Price Home Can I Qualify For?

> Vision is the art of seeing the invisible.
> *Jonathan Swift*

We all can find beautiful homes in great neighborhoods that we would enjoy living in. Of course, our ability to make the down payment and monthly payments will probably limit us to more modest homes than our dream home. (Look at your home purchase as a stepping stone to your dream home.) The key issues are our earning power, our debts and our assets to support the down payment and monthly payments.

You can get a rough estimate of the price range of homes that you can support by talking with a professional loan officer or a professional real estate agent. The following example will give you some perspective on the approach they will frequently use.

Just as an example, suppose you and your spouse have gross monthly income together of $4,000 (that is before any federal or state taxes). You may recall

"I'M MOVING"

from the chapter – The Economy – that the government calculates that 28% is the average portion of people's income that is used for housing. Method A for estimating your maximum supportable monthly payment for principal and interest plus taxes and insurance is to multiply $4,000 x 0.28 = $1,120.

$1,120

$940

Method B has a slightly different approach and takes into consideration your debt, which is considered to be long-term debt (i.e. will still be owed more than 10 months from now). Long-term debt examples are car payments at $200 per month and a VISA bill average each month of $300, for a total of $500 per month.

In Method B, the gross monthly income of $4,000 is multiplied by 0.36 = $1,440. Subtracting the $500 of monthly long-term debt leaves $940 by Method B for monthly principal and interest plus taxes and insurance.

The mortgage broker's guidelines indicate that the lower of Method A and Method B should be used to determine the buyer's financial strength. In this case, they have the financial ability to support $940 per month for principal, interest, taxes and insurance since Method B showed the lower result.

Just as a way to look at these numbers, suppose the buyer can make a 5% down payment and will get a loan for the other 95%. If they can afford $940 per month total, and 8% interest, 30-year mortgage money is available to them; $940 will pay the following monthly on an Insured Conventional Loan:

> The key issues are our earning power, our debts and our assets to support the down payment and monthly payments.

Mortgage Principal and Interest	$766
Estimated Property Taxes	94
Estimated Hazard Insurance	30
Estimated Mortgage Insurance	50
Total Monthly Payment	$940

This scenario would support a purchase price of a home of approximately $110,000. The money the buyer would need to have up front to make this purchase would be about $5,500 for a down payment and about $5,200 for closing costs – about $10,700 total.

This scenario is only provided as one example. Different down payments will change the calculations. If the buyer qualifies as a veteran, it is possible to obtain a loan from the Veteran's Administration (VA) with no down payment. Conventional loans with a 20% or more down payment currently don't require the $50 per month estimated extra mortgage insurance. Federal Housing Authority (FHA) loans have their set of costs but do offer a low down payment. VA and FHA loans have significant up front expenses, which a real estate agent can estimate for you and a mortgage company can explain in detail. The calculation formulas are subject to change so you should consult a mortgage broker.

I hope this example will give you an appreciation of the general calculation technique which is used to determine the price of the home for which you can qualify to purchase.

"I'M MOVING"

FINANCIAL ISSUES

17

Mortgages And Monthly Payments

> Do not wish to be anything but what you are, and try to be that perfectly.
> *St. Frances de Sales*

Let's start with the basics on money. You have a certain amount that you can use as a down payment. Maybe it is equity that you have accumulated over the years in your present home; maybe it is the profit you can achieve when you sell your home because your present home has increased in value over the years; maybe you have received an inheritance which you can use for a down payment, etc.

But, usually, you want a new home which costs a lot more than you can afford with your down payment nest egg. The difference in the money between the new home's selling price and your down payment (after paying the settlement fees at closing) most people obtain through a mortgage.

There are many types of mortgages and mortgage companies. But, here are a few examples of some fundamentals.

Suppose you have $30,000 to use as a down payment and you want to buy a home for $130,000. Let's look at various cases of a $100,000 mortgage to make up the difference.

"I'M MOVING"

Mortgage $100,000
30 Years
7% Interest
Monthly Payment: $665.30
Total Payments for
Principal and Interest
Over 30 Years: $239,508

Mortgage $100,000
15 Years
7% Interest
Monthly Payment: $898.83
Total Payments for
Principal and Interest
Over 15 years: $161,789

This simple example shows several key points; it is attractive to have a low monthly payment for principal and interest. However, if the payments have to be made 360 times (30 years x 12 months), the total payments are a lot more than if you can afford a somewhat higher monthly payment for 180 payments (15 years x 12 months).

Now, let's look at the difference which interest rate can make in the monthly payments and total for a 15-year mortgage.

Mortgage $100,000
15 Years
7% Interest
Monthly Payment: $898.83
Total Payments
For Principal and Interest
Over 15 years: $161,789

Mortgage $100,000
15 Years
9% Interest
Monthly Payment: $1,014.27
Total Payments
For Principal and Interest
Over 15 years: $182,569

One other simple example. Suppose you want to buy a home for $250,000 with $50,000 down payment and, therefore, need a mortgage of $200,000.

Mortgage $200,000
30 Years
7% Interest
Monthly Payment: $1,330.60
Total Payments
For Principal and Interest
Over 30 years: $479,016

Repaid Principal: $200,000
Interest: $279,016

Mortgage $200,000
15 Years
7% Interest
Monthly Payment: $1,797.66
Total Payments
For Principal and Interest
Over 15 years: $323,578

Repaid Principal: $200,000
Interest: $123,578

FINANCIAL ISSUES

To be sure, with today's tax law, the interest is tax deductible. However, the interest has to be paid before a portion can be recovered as a tax deduction.

Mortgages can be arranged through a variety of financial institutions. Your real estate agent can assist you by giving you some people to contact. Some real estate brokers own mortgage companies and their offices are in the same or nearby buildings to make the mortgage process easier for the buyer.

Building up equity in a home requires that all of the interest be paid on the unpaid balance of the mortgage and then equity can be gradually increased.

Example: A $100,000 mortgage loan at a 7% interest rate. As shown in the following table, there is a large remaining balance of $85,812 after ten (10) years of payments on a thirty (30) year loan, whereas the fifteen (15) year loan has only a $45,393 balance still due after ten (10) years. After fifteen (15) years, when the fifteen (15) year loan is all paid off, the thirty (30) year loan still has $74,019 as a balance (74% of the original loan).

$100,000 Loan: 7% Interest Rate
Remaining Balance ($)

Age of Loan	15 Year Loan	30 Year Loan
5 Years	$77,413	$94,132
10 Years	45,393	85,812
15 Years	0	74,019
20 Years		57,300
25 Years		33,599
30 Years		0

> Consider a $100,000 mortgage loan at an attractive 7% interest rate. After fifteen (15) years, when the fifteen (15) year loan is all paid off, the thirty (30) year loan still has $74,019 as a balance (74% of the original loan).

One of the many reasons people purchase a home is to build up equity. Equity is defined as Selling Price minus Mortgage. If a home sells for $125,000 and has no mortgage, the owner has $125,000 worth of equity. If the home sells for $125,000 and still has a $74,000 mortgage, as in the thirty-year loan in the case just discussed, the owner has $125,000 minus $74,000 or $51,000 worth of equity.

The 30-year loan may be attractive because of its low monthly payments. The 15-year loan is a much better way to build equity. One practical approach for the owner who is having a difficult time supporting the monthly payments initially, is to pay the 30 year loan payment each month and, whenever some money becomes available, use it to make an extra payment to reduce the principal. Over time, this approach will help accumulate equity and bring the homeowner closer to the 15-year loan scenario.

Some people move into a new home with full knowledge that they will be moving again in five (5) years or less. These short-term moves usually are related to the nature of their employment. When the time in a home will be relatively short, your mortgage banker can explain some financially attractive alternatives to the 15 and 30-year loan (for example) –

- ◆ ARM (Adjustable Rate Mortgage) or
- ◆ Balloon Loan with low initial payments.

# 18
Shopping For A Mortgage

> To be what we are, and to become what we are capable of becoming, is the only end of life.
> *Robert Louis Stephenson*

Sometimes we shop for a home first; sometimes it makes sense to shop for mortgage money first and get a pre-approval letter on a loan.

If you already have a home and some equity, it may be most appropriate to first find a real estate agent and review the homes which may suit your needs.

However, if you are renting now and considering buying your first home, or your finances are tight for buying a new home, you may be well advised to first find out how much money a qualified lender would be willing to lend you toward the purchase of a home. With that information in hand, you will be in a very good position when you talk to real estate agents. You will be able to tell them the price range of the home for which you are financially qualified and go on from there to find the ideal home.

Some real estate agents are comfortable in helping you with this financing analysis, others are not. Some real estate brokers actually own mortgage companies and are very happy to do some analysis with you free of charge.

It is often wise to get a second (or third) opinion. Mortgage bankers can provide this help as can, mortgage brokers, commercial banks and savings and loan associations. You can contact them directly, or if you want some advice on who to contact, a real estate agent will be very willing to help you.

Expect that they will ask you questions about your personal financial status. This is the only way they can do a good analysis. They will want to know your total family income, your assets, such as stock, savings, life insurance cash value, and your debts on your car, home, charge accounts, alimony, and your credit history. Do not be surprised if they ask for your last two or three years of income tax returns. All of this information will be confidential.

You will learn a lot about mortgage alternatives. Ask about FHA, VA, conventional and insured conventional mortgages; one of these is probably better than the others FOR YOU AT THIS TIME.

A home is most people's largest single investment. Mortgages are the way almost everyone makes it possible to get into a home. First homes or second homes are very important emotionally and financially. If you get off on a good foot with a mortgage, which makes sense for you, you will look back in 10, 20 and 30 years and thank that mortgage advisor and/or real estate agent who helped you.

Our financial well being is important. Before a serious operation, we are well advised to get the opinion of several physicians. When shopping for a mortgage (even before shopping for a home), talking to knowledgeable real estate agents and advisors at two (or three) mortgage companies is time well spent.

FINANCIAL ISSUES

More is better. Life isn't all about money but we can find a lot of ways to make life more enjoyable when we have some money to spend or give away.

Over the rainbow is more fun. The pot of gold isn't always at the end of the rainbow, but at least the process of seeking and following the image of the rainbow is emotionally uplifting.

Now is better than later. Now is a good time to have health and happiness and some money would also be helpful; $100 now is more valuable than $100 two years from now because we can use it to spend for our enjoyment or to earn more.

Enjoy the pleasure of giving more than receiving. Life has its givers and its takers. In the long run, those who graciously give to others reap a great emotional return on their efforts.

You are the real value behind your money. More than anything, your family wants to have time with you. Time is really the most precious commodity we have to share with others.

"I'm Moving"

19

Sales Commissions

> Most people are about as happy as they make up their minds to be.
> *Abraham Lincoln*

We are accustomed to certain practices in business. We know that a waitperson in a restaurant or a taxi driver receives a very low wage and tips are very important to their income. We have learned that 15% to 20% is a reasonable tip for good service.

Lawyers generally are compensated by the hour. However, some lawyers are willing to take the risk of investing their time for a percent of the settlement. In those cases, they get zero if they lose and about 30% of the settlement if they win the case.

When we purchase a car, we recognize that the salespeople are generally on commission for most of their compensation. They try hard to please us because they only receive a commission when the car is sold.

In most of our experiences, we appreciate a good salesperson who listens to our needs, works hard to fill our needs, and meets our personal expectations. We want the service. The salesperson wants to provide excellent service and expects to be reasonably compensated.

Commissions in real estate are the primary way that sales agents and brokers are compensated. In fact, they start out with expenses of their own:

car, advertising, an office, telephone and travel expense, etc. Then, when they sell a home, the commission is divided four ways.
1. The agent who lists the home for sale,
2. The broker of the agent who lists the home,
3. The agent who sells the home and
4. The broker of the agent who sells the home.

All commissions are negotiated between the broker and the client and are usually paid to the listing broker by the seller from their proceeds on the sale. An example of a $7,000 gross commission on a $100,000 selling price might go like this:

◆ 45% of the 7% total commission (i.e. 3.15% of the selling price) goes to the sales agent and their broker to split for finding the buyer, touring them to many appropriate homes, negotiating for them, assisting them in finding mortgage money, working with them through the details of closing, etc. (The 3.15% is split between the broker and the selling agent. In the example which follows, 60% to the sales agent and 40% to the broker).

◆ 55% of the 7% total commission (i.e. 3.85% of the selling price) goes to the listing agent and their broker. The listing includes a market analysis, helping the seller set a price which will be competitive and helping the seller complete the sale in a reasonable amount of time. Also, the listing broker and agent provide a comprehensive marketing and advertising plan, including participation in the Multiple Listing Service (MLS) and help with the details of closing.

To understand these numbers a little more, let's take the example of a home with a $100,000 Selling Price and a 7% total commission paid by the seller. The commissions will be split as follows:

Total Commission: 7% of $100,000 Selling Price **$7,000**

◆ 45% to the agent and broker who found the buyer for the property

　◆ 45% x 7% = 3.15%
　◆ 3.15% of $100,000 = $3,150

　◆ Selling agent – about 60% of $3,150　　$1,890
　◆ Selling broker – about 40% of $3,150　　$1,260
　　(Net for agent and broker will be this commission minus their expenses in providing the services – office, car, administration, etc.)

◆ 55% to the agent and broker who listed the home for the seller
(very frequently a different company than the representative for the buyer)
　◆ 55% x 7% = 3.85%
　◆ 3.85% of $100,000 = $3,850
　◆ Listing agent – 60% of $3,850　　$2,310
　◆ Listing broker – 40% of $3,850　　$1,540
　　(Net for agent and broker will be this commission minus their expenses in providing the services – advertising, office, car, administration, etc.).

There are cases where an agent works very hard for a buyer for four full days and then the buyer ends up buying a home via another agent. The four days of time and expenses must be absorbed by that agent with no compensation. That's the world of commission sales.

Let's look for a WIN-WIN solution. Interview several agents. Find one who listens well and who you feel you can TRUST; one who presents you with an excellent understanding of the market to meet your needs. Now, you have a trusting partnership or relationship and both parties are comfortable working with each other toward the goal of meeting your housing needs. Then, you sign an agreement with that agent to work together.

Commissions are the way people are paid to work in real estate. Whatever commissions they receive on completed transactions are used to pay their expenses. After expenses, what is left is now subject to Federal and State taxes just like people who receive salaries or wages. Then, what's left is for them to spend for their personal housing, food, leisure, health expenses, children's education, retirement plans, etc.

> We appreciate a good sales person who listens to our needs, works hard to fill our needs, and meets our personal expectations.

Real estate is a profession, which has many risks for the brokers and agents. If they do an excellent job for the clients, they are fairly compensated via commissions like those used in the approximate numbers described.

Real estate agents and brokers have no hourly guarantees but rather are compensated by commissions. All commissions are negotiable and different commission rates and levels of service are available.

20

Roger's Remodeling Adventure

An old home can be a gem or a gigantic problem. The price is often quite low for an old home which is in need of major repairs. But, it takes a sense of adventure and a lot of hard work to update an old home. Roger loves

> Happiness is not a state to arrive at, but a manner of traveling.
>
> Margaret Lee Runbeck

adventures and tackled the major overhaul of a home.

The kitchen needed updating with new appliances and new cabinets. When layers and layers of wallpaper were removed from the walls and ceiling of the kitchen, a section of burned out 2 x 4's was uncovered. Apparently there had been an electrical fire at one time in the past.

The back porch was falling down, but after a newly designed deck was built to replace the back porch, the backyard vista became beautiful.

Several layers of linoleum were removed and beautiful wood floors were discovered underneath. Dirty and badly worn wall-to-wall carpeting was removed and more beautiful wood flooring was found. After refinishing, the floors became a focus of elegance for the remodeled home.

The furnace needed a major overhaul. The electrical system needed upgrading. Windows and woodwork needed major sanding, repairing and repainting. Bathroom water leaks from the second floor down to the first

"I'm Moving"

required new tile and repair of one bathroom.

Outside concrete repair was needed; several trees and shrubs that had overgrown the home had to be removed. Sanding of all woodwork and new fresh paint made the exterior sparkle. The chimney needed repair and the roof needed significant repair.

During all the renovation of this four-bedroom home, Roger rented out space to three of his friends to help pay some of the expenses. The rent was reasonable but they had to tolerate the extensive inconveniences of construction. When the home was sold, the new owners paid a fair market price, which gave Roger a very nice profit after four years of renovation and simultaneous enjoyment by Roger and his three friends. The profit many people would call "sweat equity." The new owner was delighted to find the work all done. They didn't want to tackle all of the repairs, but they were willing to pay for the final product – a home with character and style, newly updated.

There are Rogers and Marilyns who love to tackle a home with character in a nice neighborhood that needs a lot of repair. After the repair, the Rogers and Marilyns often live in the home for a long time enjoying their labor of love; but, sometimes they sell and move on.

The key to enjoying this process is to visualize the end result and enjoy the step-by-step progress in the adventure. For those who have the adventuresome spirit, this is joy. For many people, this would be a cruel punishment.

PEACE-OF-MIND is a desirable goal in moving. Each of us defines what will lead to our PEACE-OF-MIND. We make our own choices.

21
The Title And Title Insurance

> Nothing in life is to be feared. It is only to be understood.
> *Madam Curie*

Suppose you have purchased a home and five years later you find out that you do not have a clear title to the property. Revolting, but possible.

Think of a home that is 80-years old and was built on a section of a subdivided farm. Over the years, land has been bought and sold a number of times; the home has been repaired and updated. Perhaps a 20-acre tract of land included the home and now there are 40 homes on the 20 acres. What could go wrong?

1. Liens for unpaid taxes or assessments over the years are judged to be your responsibility as the current owner, or
2. Unfiled or defective legal documents are found (including forgery or fraud), or
3. People go to court and claim that they are the rightful heirs of the property or
4. Deed is found to have been improperly modified.

"I'm Moving"

Prior to closing, a title search must be conducted. The purpose of title insurance is to protect the buyer and the lender should anything negative, such as the things listed above, be missed in the title search. If an unexpected problem develops, the title insurance will save you from major expenses. It is a one-time charge and covers you for as long as you own the home.

It is wise to discuss the subject of title insurance with your lender and your real estate advisor. My opinion would be, paraphrasing American Express Card's slogan, Don't Go To Closing Without It!!

Insurance

To be absolutely sure in the financial world

would be such a thrill, but it is not to be.

We can't be sure how long we may live, so

there is life insurance to help our family should we die.

We have car insurance to help us to avoid the major expense

that could result from an accident.

We have homeowner's insurance and title insurance,

because we want to be sure to avoid major expenses.

Insurance is a peculiar product.

We are happy we have it when it's needed and

even happier when we don't need to use it at all.

Financial Issues

Consider the insurance salesperson;
you are happy she sold you the insurance
when you end up needing it.
When you see her and all is going well,
you are also happy you didn't need the insurance.
Insurance is like a visit to the dentist;
we are happy when we don't need it.
Now, health insurance is a special case. We want
the coverage but how we can
complain about the complicated paperwork,
the co-pays, the deductibles, the
bills from the lab, the physician,
the hospital, the X-ray specialist, etc.
We wouldn't want to live without Social Security
and its help to us in our
senior years, it is insurance which
we pay into for many years and
at retirement appreciate.
Insurance is far from perfect, but it
helps us avoid bigger anxieties in the financial world.

"I'M MOVING"

22

The Wisdom Of A Home Inspection

Buyers of a home are extremely well advised by their real estate agents and mortgage companies to have a professional home inspection of the home they are purchasing. A comprehensive written report of any problems is well worth the cost which ranges from $250 to $500. A comprehensive home inspection should take two to three hours and the client should try to attend. As a reference point, if you were buying a 1968 vintage car for $110,000, would you consider it a good idea to take it to a reputable mechanic for a thorough checkup first? Of course.

> You will find as you look back upon your life that the moments when you have really lived, are the moments when you have done things in a spirit of love.
> Henry Drummond

The wisdom: before closing, be very sure that you understand the mechanical or maintenance or other problems with the home. Again, it is for your PEACE-OF-MIND.

To assure the professionalism of your home inspector, you should get several references and stay away from inspectors who also fix and repair homes. Check that the company has liability and errors and omissions insurance. Then, you have recourse if they miss something that costs you money. Check that they are members of ASHI (American Society of Home Inspectors) which has membership standards and a code of ethics. A detailed report should be provided by the inspector. The inspection should cover up to 1,600 items, including:

- roofing, flashing, chimneys
- exterior
- structure/foundation
- electrical system/heat pump
- cooling system/heat pump
- insulation
- plumbing
- interior
- water heater
- property and site
- major appliances

The following tables will be useful to you as residential construction remodeling estimates.

Source: Pillar to Post® Professional Home Inspection (The estimates that follow include the supply and installation of average building materials.
A typical three-bedroom home has been used as the model. Note: Costs will vary by region as well as by upgrade selections, complexity of the job itself and disposal fees.)

Structure/Exterior

Structure
*	addition (foundation to roof)	$75-$110/sq.ft
*	basement entrance	$6,000-$10,000
*	basement main beam	$1,500
*	basement support post/foundation	$300
*	excavation/waterproofing	$90-$110/sq.ft.
*	foundation cracks (excavation method)	$300-$700
*	foundation cracks (injection method)	$350
*	lintel (masonry wall)	$600
*	lower basement	$125-$300/lin.ft.
*	remove bearing wall	$2,500
*	remove partition wall	$600-$1,600
*	replace roof sheathing	$5.00-$6.00/sq.ft.
*	re-support floor joist (sistering)	$200-$300
*	underpinning	$200-$300/lin.ft.
*	termite prevention (chemical soil treatment)	$1,200+

Wall System
*	aluminum siding	$4.50/sq.ft.
*	brick veneer	$13/sq.ft.
*	brick cleaning (unpainted)	$2.50/sq.ft.
*	brick cleaning (painted)	$5.50/sq.ft.
*	brick repointing	$3.00-$7.00/sq.ft.
*	cedar siding	$6.00-$9.00/sq.ft.
*	stucco	$8-$11sq.ft.
*	vinyl siding	$3.50/sq.ft.

Exterior Door
*	aluminum storm door	$350
*	metal insulated door	$700
*	patio door - replace	$700-$1,500
*	patio door - brick wall (6 ft.)	$2,500-$3,500
*	patio door - wood wall (6 ft.)	$2,000-$3,000

Roof/Eave/Flashing/Chimney

Sloped Roofs
* asphalt shingle (over existing) — $1.75/sq.ft.
* asphalt shingle (strip and reshingle) — $2.50/sq.ft.
* asphalt shingle (high quality) — $3.00/sq.ft.
* cedar shake — $8-$10/sq.ft.
* cedar shingle — $8.50/sq.ft.
* clay tile — $10-$20/sq.ft.
* slate tile — $30-$50/sq.ft.

Flat Roofs
* roll roofing asphalt (90 lb.) — $1.00-$2.00/sq.ft.
* 4-ply (tar and gravel) — $4.00-$6.00/sq.ft.
* single ply membrane — $4.00-$6.00/sq.ft.

Gutters
* gutter cleaning — $100
* gutter/downspout – aluminum — $3.00-$4.00/lin.ft.
* gutter/downspout – galvanized — $2.75-$3.50/lin.ft.
* downspout extension — $15
* soffits/fascia (aluminum) — $10/lin.ft.

Flashing
* chimney flashing (sloped asphalt) — $200-$400
* chimney flashing (flat built-up) — $300-$500
* metal cricket at chimney — $200-$400
* parapet wall flashing — $25/lin.ft.
* roof vent — $50
* skylight — $400
* valley flashing — $15.00-$25.00/lin.ft.
* wall flashing — $3.00-$4.00/lin.ft.

Chimney
* chimney extension — $100-$250/lin.ft.
* chimney repointing — $5-$10/brick
* concrete cap (single flue) — $100-$250
* concrete cap (double flue) — $200-$350
* rain cap — $75
* re-line flue (stainless steel) — $30-$40/lin.ft.

Garage/Driveway/Walkway

Garage
* detached carport — $4,000+
* detached wood frame – single — $8,000+
* detached wood frame – double — $13,000+
* detached block – single — $18,000+
* detached block – double — $24,000+
* removal of existing garage — $1,500+

Overhead Doors
* automatic garage door opener — $350
* cladboard – single — $450-$650
* cladboard – double — $750-$1,000
* metal – single (one piece) — $700
* metal – double (one piece) — $1,100
* wood – single (sectional) — $900
* wood – double (sectional) — $1,300

Driveway
* asphalt paving (existing base) — $2.00-$3.00/sq.ft.
* asphalt paving (new base) — $3.00-$3.50/sq.ft.
* asphalt (seal) — $50-$75
* concrete (stamped) — $10-$15/sq.ft.
* interlock brick/stone — $8-$10/sq.ft.

Landscaping/Deck/Patio/Fence

Landscaping
* lay soil and sod — $1.00-$2.00/sq.ft.
* sprinkler system — $1,000
* retaining wall – concrete — $35/sq.ft.
* retaining wall – wood — $25/sq.ft.

Deck
* cedar/pressure treated — $20/sq.ft.
* custom designed and built — $15-$25/sq.ft.

Patio
* concrete (stamped) — $10-$15/sq.ft.
* flagstone/fieldstone — $16/sq.ft.
* interlock brick/stone — $8-$10/sq.ft.
* patio stone — $3.00/sq.ft.

"I'M MOVING"

Porch
* flooring — $5.00/lin.ft.
* railing — $150
* skirting — $15/lin.ft.
* steps – concrete — $400
* steps – wood — $250

Fence
* chain-link (4 ft.) — $10/sq.ft.
* wood – cedar (5 ft.) — $30/lin.ft.
* wood – pressure treated (5 ft.) — $20/lin.ft.
* reset post in concrete — $60/post

Interior

Windows
* awning — $50/sq.ft.
* bay — $45/sq.ft.
* casement — $50/sq.ft.
* double hung — $45/sq.ft.
* skylight/roof window — $2,600+
* slider – aluminum — $30/sq.ft.
* storm – aluminum — $100-$200
* thermal glass (existing frame) — $25/sq.ft.
* replacement aluminum sliders — $25/sq.ft.
* replacement awning/casement — $50/sq.ft.
* replacement double hung — $35-$45/sq.ft.

Ceiling/Wall
* acoustic ceiling (suspended) — $4.00/sq.ft.
* baseboard/door/window casing — $2.50/lin.ft.
* drywall over plaster — $2.00/sq.ft.
* plaster (over existing plaster) — $3.50/sq.ft.
* stucco/stipple — $1.00/sq.ft.
* walls (insulation, drywall) — $2.50/sq.ft.
* walls painting (3 coats) — $1.25/sq.ft.
* wallpaper — $2.00-$8.00/sq.ft.

Floor
* carpet – clean — $35-$50/room
* carpet – indoor/outdoor — $1.50/sq.ft.
* carpet and underpad — $4.00/sq.ft.
* ceramic tile — $15/sq.ft.
* finished subfloor — $3.50/sq.ft.
* hardwood – 3/8" — $5.00-$7.00/sq.ft.
* hardwood – 3/4" — $8-$10/sq.ft.

Financial Issues

- * hardwood – parquet — $6.00/sq.ft.
- * hardwood – sand and refinish — $1.50-$3.00/sq.ft.
- * vinyl – sheet — $8-$12/sq.ft.
- * vinyl – tile — $1.00-$2.50/sq.ft.

Interior Door
- * closet – louver — $150-$250
- * closet – mirror — $800
- * custom with casing/hardware — $400
- * hollow-core — $200
- * french — $700

Stairs/Railings
- * circular stair – oak — $1,700
- * circular stair – carpet — $1,200
- * standard stair – oak — $1,250
- * standard stair – carpet — $700
- * stair railing — $60-$90/lin. ft.

Insulation
- * rigid exterior (prior to finish) — $1.00-$2.00/sq.ft.
- * R20 (6") of loose — $0.75-$1.25/sq.ft.
- * R32 (10") of loose — $1.00-$1.50/sq.ft.
- * wall/roof cavity — $1.50-$3.00/sq.ft.
- * UFFI removal — $20-$35/sq.ft.

Fireplaces
- * damper — $250-$500
- * brick replacement — $300-$500
- * gas insert — $2,500-$3,500
- * glass door — $200
- * hearth extension — $250
- * flue cleaning — $90
- * metal box insert — $700-$1,200
- * masonry (with flue rough-in) — $2,500
- * wood stove — $1,500-$2,500

Kitchen/Bathroom
- * kitchen cabinet — $200/lin.ft.
- * kitchen counter — $20/lin.ft.
- * kitchen renovation — $8,000+
- * bathroom renovation — $6,000+

Security System
* alarm monitoring — $20/month
* alarm system — $2,500
* intercom system (retrofit) — $1,200
* wired system — $1,300
* wireless motion detectors — $500

Miscellaneous
* central vacuum (retrofit) — $800-$1,000
* central vacuum (canister only) — $800-$1,000

Swimming Pool/Hot Tub

* pool – vinyl lined (15 ft. x 30 ft.) — $15,000+
* pool – concrete lined (15 ft. x 30 ft.) — $30,000+
* pool heater — $1,500
* pump/filter — $1,200
* hot tub fiberglass — $3,500-$4,500

Electrical

Retrofit
* attic ventilator – mechanical — $250
* baseboard heater — $150-$200
* ceiling fan — $200
* doorbell system — $80-$100
* dryer duct — $100-$150
* electric smoke detector — $60-$80
* exhaust fan – bathroom — $135-$150
* exhaust fan – oven — $200-$250
* exterior light fixture — $100-$250
* fluorescent light fixture — $150-$250
* ground – public system — $75-$100
* ground – private system (with ground rods) — $200-$300
* receptacle – conventional — $100-$150
* receptacle – split — $150-$250
* receptacle – exterior with cover — $150-$250
* receptacle – replace conventional with GFCI — $70
* receptacle – CO/ALR (aluminum) — $15
* receptacle – stove/dryer — $75-$100
* receptacle – rewire reverse polarity — $10
* standard light fixture — $100-$200
* switch (existing wiring) — $10-$20

Upgrade
* 100 amp (new panel) — $900-$1,300
* 100 amp (existing panel) — $500-$800
* 200 amp (new panel) — $1,800-$2,000
* 200 amp (existing panel) — $1,000-$1,200
* breaker panel – main — $400-$600
* breaker panel – auxiliary — $100-$300
* replace circuit breaker (to 20 amp) — $75
* 120/240 volt circuit — $200-$300

Heating/Cooling

Forced-Air System
* air duct (new) — $3,500
* air duct (retrofit) — $5,500
* annual service — $50
* blower/motor — $300-$500
* clean duct — $150-$300
* convert oil to gas (1 story) — $2,000-$3,000
* convert hot water to forced air (1 story) — $9,000
* electronic air filter — $500-$900
* gas – mid efficiency — $2,000-$2,800
* gas – high efficiency — $2,700-$3,500
* humidifier – drum type — $75-$150
* humidifier – flow through type — $350-$450
* metal line existing chimney flue — $500-$1,000

Hot Water System
* circulating pump — $500-$750
* cast iron radiator (basement) — $450-$650
* expansion tank — $250-$300
* gas boiler – standard — $2,500-$3,500
* gas boiler – high efficiency — $3,500-$5,000
* removal of oil tank — $350-$500
* radiator/boiler removal — $1,500-$2,000
* radiator — $500-$900
* radiator valve — $100

Air Conditioner/Heat Pump
* air handler 3-ton (vertical) — $1,200-$1,500
* air handler 3-ton (horizontal) — $1,500-$1,800
* window unit — $700-$1,000
* central A/C – existing duct — $1,500-$3,000
* central A/C – attic mounted; separate duct — $9,000
* condensate pump — $130
* heat recovery ventilator (HRV) — $1,500-$2,500
* heat pump — $4,500-$6,000

"I'M MOVING"

Plumbing

Bathroom
* basin – pedestal — $300
* basin – vanity — $200
* bathtub – replace/retile — $1,900
* shower connection — $200
* shower stall – plastic — $700-$1,900
* shower stall – retile — $1,700-$2,500
* toilet – flush mechanism — $100-$150
* toilet – replace — $350
* toilet – replace seal — $100-$250
* toilet – unclog — $100-$200
* tub enclosure – ceramic tile — $1,200
* tub enclosure – plastic — $300-$400
* whirlpool bath/faucet — $3,500

Kitchen
* dishwasher – install — $550-$800
* dishwasher – replace — $400-$650
* garbage disposal — $300-$500
* sink – single — $300
* sink – double — $400
* sink – replace — $400-$550
* vegetable sprayer — $50

Private Plumbing System
* laundry tub and waste pump — $250-$350
* septic tank (1,000 gals.) — $5,000-$10,000
* septic tank cleaning — $150
* sewage waste pump — $1,300-$1,700
* well – shallow — $25/lin.ft.
* well – deep — $35/lin. ft.
* well – submersible pump — $1,000
* well – suction/jet pump — $500-$900

Upgrade
* hose bib — $100-$150
* hot water tank (40 gal. – electric) — $500-$700
* laundry tub/connection — $300-$500
* main water service — $150-$200/lin.ft.
* main shut-off valve — $150-$300
* sump pump — $150-$250
* supply lines – 1 story; up to 2 baths — $1,200-$2,500
* supply lines – 2 story; up to 2 baths — $2,000-$3,000
* water softener — $800-$1,500
* waste drain lines — $1,500-$3,000

LIFE EXPECTANCY

Component	Average Life (Yrs)
Roof Covering	
* asphalt standard shingle	12-15
* asphalt premium shingle	15-30
* wood shingle	10-20
* cement tile	20-40
* asbestos cement	40-80
* slate tile	40-80
* roll roofing	5-15
* tar and gravel	15-25
* metal	60
Heating	
* forced air furnace	10-25
* oil tank	40
* water/steam boiler – welded steel	15-30
* water/steam boiler – cast iron	30-50
* water/steam circulating pump	10-25
Cooling	
* central air	10-15
* heat pump	10-15
* window – air conditioning	10-20
Plumbing	
* galvanized water pip	20-25
* hot water heater	5-15
* septic/sewer pump	5-10
* well pump	10
Appliances	
* dishwasher	5-12
* dryer	10-25
* garbage disposal	5-12
* oven/range	15-20
* washing machine	5-15

Your real estate agent can counsel you on the steps to be taken prior to closing based on the details in The Home Inspection Report.

FINANCIAL ISSUES

"I'M MOVING"

MORE EMOTIONAL ISSUES

23. MICHELLE MOVES TO FLORIDA
24. TEARS OF SADNESS AND JOY
25. WHAT IS YOUR WORK? IS IT REAL ESTATE?
26. RETIREMENT COMMUNITIES, ETC.
27. DIVORCE AND MOVING
28. WHAT'S IMPORTANT IN LIFE ANYHOW?

23
Michelle Moves To Florida

> Where there is love, there is life.
> *Mohandas Gandhi*

The Johnson family is moving to Florida and Michelle is not a bit happy. Her Mom got a great new job offer in Florida and her Dad is willing to find a new job in Florida also. Mom and Dad are pleased with the move from Colorado to Florida but Michelle, age 14, is not at all happy. Actually, she is very upset; Mom and Dad have never experienced Michelle being so upset.

Let's ask Michelle. "It's just not fair," she said. "I've got some great friends and I just don't feel good about leaving my friends and starting all over with new friends in Florida. I'm on the swimming team and track team and I don't know if I would make those teams in Florida. Mom and Dad just don't understand my point of view."

The teen-age years are tough psychologically for moving. Friends, peer pressure, adjusting

"I'M MOVING"

> The teenage years are tough psychologically for moving. Friends, peer pressure, adjusting to new hormones, learning to set standards and limits and values.

to new hormones, learning to set standards and limits and values. It is a difficult time of life with many pressures and teenagers can't be expected to be enthusiastic about the perceived and real stress of moving.

So, what's a parent to do? Both parents love Michelle and want the best for her. Now, they see a conflict between meeting Michelle's desires and theirs. Every family will handle this situation in their own way. After a lot of discussion, they agree to have Michelle take a trip to Florida with Mom and Dad as they check out their jobs and a place to live. Many personal issues are resolved and they agree to put their home up for sale in May and look for a new home in Florida to move into in August so Michelle can start school in September.

Now the plot thickens. The Johnsons find a home in Florida, but the home in Colorado isn't selling. They can't afford two monthly payments, so what can they do? Michelle, as you might expect, volunteers to stay in the Colorado home until it sells and, will continue in her Colorado school. Mom's new boss in Florida wants her to be there full time starting July 15th. Dad doesn't quite know when he should give notice on his present job and work hard finding a Florida job.

Time slips by and the closing on the Florida home is finally scheduled for August 1st, but the Colorado home hasn't sold yet.

This is not a far-fetched situation. This has happened to many people moving to a new place.

More Emotional Issues

The goal is Peace-of-Mind; this situation is not leading to Peace-of-Mind for the Johnsons. Let's think through the scenario and look for ways that the Johnsons and their real estate agents might have reduced the anxiety.

One area for negotiation is Mom Johnson with her boss. Mom Johnson perhaps could have accepted the Florida job with a clear understanding that she had to have her Colorado home sold before starting full time in Florida. Mom Johnson is in a good negotiating position because she is getting an excellent job and the company wants her.

A second area of negotiation is the Johnsons with their real estate agent and the agent for the owners of the home for which the August 1st closing is scheduled. Maybe the sellers of the Florida home will be willing to delay closing 30 to 60 days. A lot depends on their next home move, and also, a lot depends on the wording of the Purchase Agreement which the Johnsons signed. Did it have a strong contingency related to the sale of their Colorado home?

A third area of negotiation is potentially with the real estate agent and their broker who is selling their home in Colorado. Was the price established originally too high for the market to assure a prompt sale? Should the price be reduced now? Should the Johnsons change to a new real estate agent and broker? Again, it depends on how good a job was done on setting a realistic selling price on the Colorado home. Did the agent and broker have a good marketing plan and did they fully execute it – advertising, open houses, tours with agents, etc? And what does the Listing Agreement say about how the Agreement can be terminated? Also, can the Colorado home be rented for a few months?

Every situation is different. However, to assure PEACE-OF-MIND,

"I'M MOVING"

or at least have a high probability of PEACE-OF-MIND, it is extremely important to:
1. Select real estate agents very carefully.
2. Communicate with them often and expect them to meet their marketing plan.
3. Update the plan. If a home isn't sold in 30 days, the number of people who will tour it will likely decrease in the second month. After 30 to 60 days, at the longest, the price should be reconsidered, or the promotion program changed, or something.

Since the Johnson story is only an example, there is no conclusion as to how it ends. The ending is always more likely to be a happy ending if you pay attention every step along the way. There are no guarantees that any one plan will work, but for the Johnsons, working extremely closely and creatively with their real estate agents in both Florida and Colorado will probably lead to a successful outcome.

Michelle found herself in the middle of a moving problem. When she has to face moving problems in her life in the future, we hope her Mom and Dad have set a good example for her that led to PEACE-OF-MIND during the potentially very emotionally difficult move.

24

Tears Of Sadness And Joy

> After the verb "to love," "to help" is the most beautiful verb in the world.
>
> Bertha von Suttner

"I'm moving and I'm crying. There are so many sad things about moving. I've put so much time into working on my yard, planting flowers and shrubs. Every room in my home needed painting or wallpaper. The refrigerator had to be replaced. We needed more furniture to make the home comfortable. So, now that the home is in pretty nice shape, I'm moving. I sit down and cry. I'll miss my friends in this neighborhood."

"Why am I moving anyhow? Oh, I realize why – changing family needs, a new job position, a larger family, a smaller family now, etc. But I'm still sad about moving, so I cry occasionally."

"The good news is, I'm happy with my new situation. There are some exciting things about the new adventure of moving to a new home. It's an opportunity to fine-tune the new home to my latest definition of my needs. I always wanted a larger kitchen, but the remodeling costs would have been huge on the old home. I can get the large kitchen I want by selecting a new home with a great kitchen. I've always wanted to live in a wooded area. It wasn't possible with my old

"I'M MOVING"

home, but it will be one of my specifications with my new home. Now, when I reflect on it, my tears can be tears of joy. I'm excited about the thought of my new home."

Tears Of Sadness And Joy

Tears come to my eyes at weddings when

I am so happy for the bride and groom,

The emotions of joy and happiness just

naturally trigger the tear ducts to generate tears,

Tears, what a wonderful signal that our

lives are rich with emotions.

A chorus can sing a beautiful song

and my tears begin to flow,

A movie can have a touching scene of love or

compassion and the tear ducts go to work,

What a wonder that our tears can originate with

the emotions of joy, happiness, love or compassion.

But what of sadness and tears?

The same tear ducts generate tears

from the stimulus of sadness.

At a funeral, we cry when our brain is wrestling with the

relationship that was and the new reality of death.

Years after a time of sadness, if we focus our thoughts on the

sad incident, our emotions go to work and the tears flow.

A broken relationship is a sad happening and tears

remind us of what might have been.

Those who have cried often have lived richly.

To not have cried is to have controlled the

emotions so much as to deny their reality.

Tears are a great cleanser.

They cleanse the eyes and the soul.

Tears are a wonderful gift –

tears of sadness and joy; tears of a full rich life.

"I'M MOVING"

25

What Is Your Work? Is It Real Estate?

> Man's mind, once stretched by a new idea, never regains its original dimensions.
> *Oliver Wendell Holmes*

If you earn your living as a barber, you have been trained and your clients enjoy the benefits of your skill. Doctors are trained. Lawyers are trained. They take tests and are approved by professional associations and often government authorities to practice their profession in certain states.

Real estate agents and real estate brokers are licensed by the State after training and testing. They also must have continuing education at least every two years to maintain their licenses. They follow government-mandated rules. Often brokers and agents join the Realtors® Association, thereby agreeing to abide by the code of ethics.

Buyers and sellers of homes have other jobs where they earn their money. An administrative assistant, plumber, salesperson or accountant may be very good at their jobs but they do not understand the details of being a barber, doctor, lawyer or real estate agent. Each person decides when it is most prudent to hire the services of others. It works because we respect the knowledge of others; we cannot know everything in all fields.

Reflections On Work

The farmer works hard in his fields and the harvest is good.
The rain and sun from the heavens have
blessed the farmer's work
and the results are satisfying to the farmer, to his family,
and to society.
Surely this has been important work, and the farmer
has made a major contribution.
And, in the satisfaction of a job well done,
the farmer is at peace,
And in harmony with this work and the result.
When our work is an important part of our purpose in life,
to love and to be loved, we can truly love our work.
But what if we dislike our work and find
it unsatisfying or even drudgery?
We need only to ask ourselves,
"Is this work helping my soul, my essence,
to grow or to whither?"
If our work is not leading to peace of mind and a feeling of
satisfaction and contribution, it is our obligation to ourselves
to find other work.
Each person must decide for themselves
what type of work will be a growth mechanism for them.
To work so many hours at unsatisfying work
is not healthy for the growth of the Spirit.
To contribute to the growth of our Spirit, we need work
that is positive and useful to society.

MORE EMOTIONAL ISSUES

26
Retirement Communities, Assisted Living Communities And Long-Term Care Facilities

> All of the significant battles are waged within the self.
> Sheldon Kopp

As the years pass by, there arrives a day when a person or a couple decide that it is no longer physically or financially practical to live in their own private home. Yet, they still want a home that is safe, comfortable and nurturing.

Retirement communities are growing in popularity. They offer the many safety and social advantages of being part of a community while providing considerable independent living choices for those who want them.

If some medical care is needed, assisted living communities provide nursing and other medical services. Special programs for Alzheimer's patients (as an example) are also available in assisted living communities.

Long-term care facilities (previously called nursing homes) are the residence of many people who no longer can care for themselves and whose families cannot practically care for them either.

In the decision to move to one of these three alternatives, a real estate agent you can TRUST should also be one who has great patience and compassion.

"I'M MOVING"

Clara found herself in a situation where her husband had died and she was feeling that a retirement community might be best for her. Her minister suggested that she stay in her home for a year to work through the grief. Her family members counseled with her, discussing her wishes and all financial issues.

> It is important that we understand the emotional anxieties of people who move into one of these three alternatives. At this time, family support is absolutely essential!

A key turning point occurred when Clara began to work with a real estate agent, Martha, to sell her family home. Martha's help with the real estate details was very important, but equally as important were her patience and compassion.

It is important that we understand the emotional anxieties of people who move into one of these three alternatives. They are usually very necessary moves. At this time, family support is absolutely essential!

There is always a bright side…but it sometimes is hard for a person to accept.

Studies in long-term care facilities have shown that the positive experiences of the residents come from:
- family member visits,
- music,
- children,
- and pets.

The toes tap when there is music in the building. Some facilities hire a professional to sing and play an instrument. Choirs and volunteer musicians are always welcome.

Children bring a smile to almost every face.

Just to hug someone is a wonderful treat.

These moves are a part of the reality of living in many homes throughout our life. All moves are important to review carefully to assure our PEACE-OF-MIND.

"I'M MOVING"

27
Divorce And Moving

> We are all born for love. It is the principle of existence, and its only end.
> *Benjamin Disraeli*

Talk about emotion. With so many marriages ending in divorce, some real estate agents report that almost half of their real estate transactions directly involve a divorce.

So, if you or one of your friends find themselves in a divorce situation where the home needs to be sold, a professional real estate agent understands the emotional as well as the financial side of such a situation.

The agent isn't a therapist or a marriage counselor. He must remain objective and not take sides. But, he can be very understanding of the needs for a prompt resolution of the "problem" – getting the home sold.

Legal issues are also important. It is important for the real estate agent to know if he is working on the behalf of the husband, the wife, the ex-husband, the ex-wife or both. The home could be sold before or after the final divorce decree is official.

The real estate agent should be a person you TRUST. And once you have worked well with your real estate agent in the sale of your home, he can also help you to find a new home or apartment. Even if you are moving to a new city or state, the real estate agent can refer you to a reputable agent in your new location.

Divorce is such a difficult time emotionally that the development of the decision to sell the home, what price should be charged, what agent should be used, what broker should be used, etc. are full of difficulties. It is complicated enough when the parties are communicating well. In a divorce or soon-to-be-divorce situation, the communication is badly strained, at the very best.

Find a real estate agent you can TRUST and you will greatly increase your PEACE-OF-MIND.

> Divorce is an opportunity for our spirit to mature and grow and bring us to PEACE-OF-MIND and excitement for life's new vistas.

MORE EMOTIONAL ISSUES

Beyond Divorce

We shall live together, love and honor each other,

until death shall part us.

We fell in love, we enjoyed being with each other,

and marriage seemed so natural.

Intimacy, love and anger are all powerful emotions.

which we experienced in courtship,

marriage, and finally divorce.

When we are truly intimate and share the deepest

thoughts of our soul with our partner,

the relationship can be rich or dangerous.

Rich, if both parties are honest and commit

themselves to the marriage with

unconditional love, and

Dangerous, if one or both spouses are

playing games of power or

selfishness or manipulation.

The beauty of marriage is unconditional love,

sharing of joy and sadness,

and often, the blessings of children.

"I'M MOVING"

The tragedy of divorce is the fear and

anger that wells up in our hearts and the

hearts of our children.

We wish that unconditional love had

preserved our marriage and we wouldn't have

to experience fear and anger.

But, we must heal our hearts to go on with life.

As hard as it is, we must forgive

ourselves and forgive our divorced partner.

Our memories of good times can always

return to us in conscious, subconscious,

and unconscious thought.

When memories of bad times occur, and they do,

we need to move through

our anger to the unconditional love and forgiveness

which is our goal.

Divorce is a opportunity for our spirit

to mature and grow and

bring us to PEACE-OF-MIND and

excitement for life's new vistas.

28
What's Important In Life Anyhow?

> Life without love is like a tree without blossom and fruit.
> *Kahlil Gibran*

"Sure, there is anxiety in moving," Joan's mother told her, "but moving is just a part of life." She continued, "You'll get over the move; consider it only as INCONVENIENT; it's not the end of the world, after all."

Joan's mother said, "Let me give you one word that will help you in any problem you might have – anxiety over moving, a relationship problem, a medical problem, a financial problem...whatever. The word is INCONVENIENT. It's not a very exciting word, but it gives you a new mind set. In fact, you probably could find reasons to consider moving as a great opportunity."

My family, as I grew up, were mom, pop and sister (6-1/2 years older). I remember conferring with my sister often on what mom and pop would likely accept or reject – a bike trip, traveling to a distant swimming pool, allowance negotiations, etc. After all, older sisters should know these things – and she generally gave good advice like, "Make sure mom is in a good mood before you ask," and "Make sure the other kids also have their parent's okay."

Then one day when I was 36, my sister died of a heart attack brought on by an asthma attack. Forty-three is too young to die, mom, pop and I and all my sister's family and friends concluded.

Rabbi Kirschner's book, <u>When Bad Things Happen To Good People,</u> was very consoling at the time. A friend at work gave me the book as a gift because it had helped her so much in a time of grief. That friend touched me in a special way – she was an angel who crossed my path and was kind when I needed kindness. Her gift of the book was an act of friendship, which I have remembered many times as I have been on the same path with people in pain.

The first year after my sister's death, she was constantly in my conscious, subconscious and unconscious mind. In dreams I could see her and talk to her, even though others in the room didn't realize she was there. Her spirit and memory were within me and to this day have not departed. When I wake from a dream, which included my sister, I say, "Hallelujah."

And now my original family (mom, pop and sister) are not physically on earth but their spirits are still with me and always will be.

The message: Think carefully, what really is important in your life?

The Simple Truth

To love and be loved; is it that simple?

We ponder the miracle of our life, from the power of the Universe

to an egg, to a sperm, to our life,

Why are we here? What is our purpose in life?

What is our unique nature?

To love and be loved; is it that simple?

There is only one person that is on earth or ever was on earth

or ever will be on earth who is me, and that is the me that I am.

Is my purpose in life to own a car, or a house,

or land, or animals or forests?

Is my purpose to serve others or to manipulate situations

to serve only my own desires?

To love and be loved; is it that simple?

When we come into this life as a baby and leave

our bodily life in death, only our Spirit is the constant.

Our form has changed over the years,

our Spirit has been nurtured and grown

if we have loved and been loved.

It is that simple, our purpose in life is to love and be loved;

everything else is secondary.

"I'M MOVING"

29
Practical Exercise: A Workbook Section

> No legacy is so rich as honesty.
> William Shakespeare

Suggestion: Record your first thoughts off the top of your head quickly. Complete the next few pages in 5 to 10 minutes maximum. On factual areas, just guess at first, don't check any records. After this quick exercise, you will have the "impressions" from your mind recorded. Then, you can check facts, get other members of the family to do the exercise, discuss the pros and cons, and reach a consensus.

Let's start; yes, write in the book and do it now.

1. Selling Your Home?

            Why?   Why not?

_____

_____

_____

_____

_____

"I'm Moving"

2. What will be the likely effects on all family members?

Family Member	Positive Effects	Negative Effects

Family Member	Positive Effects	Negative Effects

Family Member	Positive Effects	Negative Effects

Family Member	Positive Effects	Negative Effects

PRACTICAL EXERCISE

Family Member	Positive Effects	Negative Effects

Family Member	Positive Effects	Negative Effects

3. What is the approximate market price range?

_____

4. What equity do we have in this home?

_____

5. Where will we live if, or when, we sell this home?

_____

Pros of new location	Cons of new location

"I'M MOVING"

_____
_____
_____

6. Who do we know who we can trust to help us in selling our home?

Real Estate Brokers

_____
_____

Real Estate Sales Agents

_____
_____

Others

_____
_____
_____

7. Are we well informed to proceed?

_____
_____
_____

PRACTICAL EXERCISE

8. If not, what steps do we need to take before proceeding?

_____
_____
_____
_____

PRACTICAL EXERCISE: A WORKBOOK SECTION

1. Buying A Home?

Why?   Why not?

_____
_____
_____
_____
_____
_____
_____
_____

2. What will be the likely effects on all family members?

Family Member   Positive Effects   Negative Effects

_____

_____

_____

_____

Family Member   Positive Effects   Negative Effects

_____

_____

_____

_____

Family Member   Positive Effects   Negative Effects

_____

_____

_____

_____

Family Member   Positive Effects   Negative Effects

_____

_____

_____

_____

Family Member	Positive Effects	Negative Effects

Family Member	Positive Effects	Negative Effects

3. **What is the approximate market price range?**

_____

4. **What equity or savings do we have to buy a new home?**

_____

5. **Where will we live until we buy a new home?**

_____

"I'm Moving"

Pros of present location   Cons of present location

_____

_____

_____

_____

6. Who do we know who we can trust to help us in buying our new home?

Real Estate Brokers

_____

_____

_____

_____

Real Estate Sales Agents

_____

_____

_____

_____

Others

_____

_____

_____

7. Are we well informed to proceed?

_____

_____

8. If not, what steps do we need to take before proceeding?

_____

_____

PRACTICAL EXERCISE – OVERVIEW

These workbook sections are not designed to cover every family issue, every work issue, every financial issue, etc. The practical exercises are designed to stimulate you and your family to think through many positives and negatives so you can proceed with a clear understanding.

PEACE-OF-MIND will come only after you have addressed the realities and are confident you are on a sound path.

Now, look over your worksheets and talk over questions with your family members, real estate professionals, etc.

It is our hope that I'M MOVING has helped you to address the many questions with a minimum of anxiety and a greater comfort that you are much more ready to move now with both your left and right brains actively involved. If so, I'M MOVING will have served its useful purpose.

SUMMARY

30. SUMMARY OF I'M MOVING

31. I'M MOVING FEEDBACK FROM READERS

32. ORDER FORM FOR MORE COPIES OF I'M MOVING

30
Summary of I'M MOVING

Six Key Thoughts

1. Moving can be a joy or very difficult emotionally and financially for you and your family.

> Destiny is not a matter of chance; it is a matter of choice.
> William Jennings Bryan

2. To eliminate the anxiety of moving and buying and/or selling a home, it is helpful to have reliable information and a real estate sales agent you have confidence in and can TRUST.

3. There is a good and a poor time to move, but when a move is necessary, you can make the best of the situation and have PEACE-OF-MIND if you develop a plan and work the plan with a real estate professional.

4. Real estate is a complicated field and you have your own profession to focus on for the good of yourself and your family.

5. Buying or selling a home is a major financial transaction, which should be studied carefully.

6. In the context of your life and its larger purpose, it may be wise to not jump to hasty conclusions on buying or selling a home. PEACE-OF-MIND is available by admitting that you can benefit emotionally and financially by employing a real estate professional to advise you on the many details involved in buying and/or selling a home.

I'M MOVING was designed as a fun book to read, but yet, it has a very serious purpose – to greatly reduce or eliminate the anxiety of moving and to lead to PEACE-OF-MIND.

We hope we have helped you in some small way to reach that goal.

SUMMARY

A Fun Word Puzzle.

Puzzle Clues	Number of Letters

Money exchanged (__) __ __ __ __

Joyous experience (__) __ __

A building for a family __ __ __ __ (__)

One who represents another (__) __ __ __ __

The absence of anxiety and fear __ __ __ (__) __

Thoughtfulness __ __ __ (__) __ __ __ __

One who purchases a home __ __ (__) __ __

One who offers their home for sale __ __ __ __ (__) __

The last word of this book's title __ (__) __ __ __ __

Stress and tension about the future __ __ __ (__) __ __ __

A loan to help purchase a home (__) __ __ __ __ __ __

Opposite of smart (__) __ __ __

The act of putting a home on the market __ __ __ __ __ (__) __

A container for moving __ (__) __

Complete confidence in another __ __ __ (__)

A vehicle for moving __ (__) __

Puzzle solution (from bracketed letters above)

__ __ __ __   __ __ __   __ __ __ __ __   __ __ __ __

161

And Finally...

On the following pages we request your feedback so that we can improve future editions of I'M MOVING. My goal has been to leave you with PEACE-OF-MIND and much less anxiety regarding your buying or selling of a home and moving; have I succeeded?

As you know, this is a different book than any book you have read before. That has been my passion! Please take a few minutes and send me the next page: "Feedback From Readers" with your comments. Thank you in advance for your help to improve future editions of I'M MOVING.

Also, there is an order form if you want to order additional copies of I'M MOVING for your friends and associates.

SUMMARY

31
I'M MOVING Feedback From Readers

(Please complete, clip out and mail to us. Thanks in advance.)

"We greatly appreciate your comments so we can improve future editions of I'M MOVING." — Bill Peter

**TO: Bill Peter & Associates
    5200 West 73rd Street
    Minneapolis, MN 55439**
FROM:
Name_____
Address _____
City, State, Zip _____
Home Phone:_____
Work Phone:_____

Comments on I'M MOVING

1. What attracted you to this book?

_____
_____
_____
_____
_____

163

"I'M MOVING"

2. Did it deliver on its promise of PEACE-OF-MIND and eliminating the anxiety of buying or selling a home?

_____
_____
_____
_____

3. What did you like best?

_____
_____
_____
_____

4. What did you like least?

_____
_____
_____
_____

5. What are your recommendations for future editions?

_____
_____
_____
_____

For more information call
us toll-free at 1-877- I'M MOVING

SUMMARY

32

Order Form For More Copies Of I'M MOVING

TO: Bill Peter & Associates
      5200 West 73rd Street
      Minneapolis, MN 55439

FROM:
Name _____
Address _____
City, State, Zip _____
Home Phone: _____
Work Phone: _____

Please mail your order to the address above along with your personal check.

Order authorized by: _____

                            Your signature

                    _____

                              Order Date

_____ Copies of I'M MOVING at $5.00 per copy   = $_____

(61% discount from $12.95 price - minimum order of 36 copies)

Shipping and Handling
(Allow 3-5 weeks for delivery)   = $ _18.00_

Total Cost (Your Personal Check Enclosed)   = $_____

                (Note: For larger orders, call toll-free
                1-877 - I'M MOVING for a price quote.)

For more information call toll free at 1-877- I'M MOVING

"I'M MOVING"

APPENDIX

33. QUOTES ON PEACE-OF-MIND
34. ABOUT THE AUTHOR

APPENDIX

33
Quotes on PEACE-OF-MIND

Courage is the price that life exacts for granting peace.
Amelia Earhart

After the verb "to love," "to help" is the most beautiful verb in the world.
Bertha von Suttner

Happiness is not a state to arrive at, but a manner of traveling.
Margaret Lee Runbeck

Most people are about as happy as they make up their minds to be.
Abraham Lincoln

Nothing in life is to be feared. It is only to be understood.
Madam Curie

Where there is love, there is life.
Mohandas Gandhi

You will find as you look back upon your life that the moments when you have really lived, are the moments when you have done things in a spirit of love.
Henry Drummond

Love is life, and if you miss love, you miss life.
Leo Buscaglia

"I'M MOVING"

People can alter their lives by altering their attitudes.
>William James

Man's mind, once stretched by a new idea, never regains its original dimensions.
>Oliver Wendell Holmes

The future belongs to those who believe in the beauty of their dreams.
>Eleanor Roosevelt

It is one of the most beautiful compensations of this life that no man can sincerely try to help another without helping himself.
>Ralph Waldo Emerson

Do not wish to be anything but what you are, and try to be that perfectly.
>St. Frances de Sales

I don't know what your destiny will be, but one thing I know, the only ones among you who will be really happy are those who will have sought and found how to serve.
>Dr. Albert Schweitzer

You will become as small as your controlling desire; as great as your dominant aspiration.
>James Allen

Vision is the art of seeing the invisible.
>Jonathan Swift

Some men see things as they are and say, "Why?" I dream of things that never were, and say, "Why not?"
>George Bernard Shaw

Appendix

It's what you learn after you know it all that counts.
John Wooden

Never, never, never quit.
Winston Churchill

One person with courage is a majority.
Andrew Johnson

All of the significant battles are waged within the self.
Sheldon Kopp

Whether you think you can or think you can't – you are right.
Henry Ford

Courage is resistance to fear, mastery of fear – not the absence of fear.
Mark Twain

Nothing splendid has ever been achieved except by those who dared believe that something inside of them was superior to circumstance.
Bruce Barton

To be what we are, and to become what we are capable of becoming, is the only end of life.
Robert Louis Stephenson

No legacy is so rich as honesty.
William Shakespeare

All our dreams can come true – if we have the courage to pursue them.
Walt Disney

"I'm Moving"

The greatest mistake a person can make is to be afraid of making one.
> Elbert Hubbard

Failure is success if we learn from it.
> Malcolm Forbes

Honesty is the first chapter of the book of wisdom.
> Thomas Jefferson

Destiny is not a matter of chance; it is a matter of choice.
> William Jennings Bryan

In the middle of difficulty lies opportunity.
> Albert Einstein

If there's a way to do it better… find it.
> Thomas Edison

We are all born for love. It is the principle of existence, and its only end.
> Benjamin Disraeli

I am imagination. I can see what the eyes cannot see. I can hear what the ears cannot hear. I can feel what the heart cannot feel.
> Peter Nivio Zarlenga

Life without love is like a tree without blossom and fruit.
> Kahlil Gibran

APPENDIX

34
About The Author

Bill Peter is a management consultant, realtor and author whose home is in Minneapolis, Minnesota.

He has lived in nineteen homes in nine states and experienced first-hand the anxiety of moving and buying and selling a home.

Also, Bill is currently completing a book on business principles for the year 2000 and beyond: <u>Unleashing business creativity......the power within your associates.</u>

"I'M MOVING"

"Eliminating the anxiety of buying or selling a home."

For information on purchasing additional copies of this book:

- *Call toll free: 1-877-I'M MOVING, or*

- *Complete the **Order Form** from Chapter 32, and mail.*

APPENDIX

DEAR "I'M MOVING" READER...

To help us improve future editions of "I'M MOVING," please send us the **Feedback From Readers** page in Chapter 31.

Thank You,

Bill Peter

"I'M MOVING"

Notes

APPENDIX

Notes